MW01273386

A different way of seeing ...

Columbia River Reader Press

Dedication

With appreciation to
Columbia River Reader readers,
whose enthusiasm and interest
over the past sixteen years
inspired and energized us to
collect and expand the original
Dispatch from the Discovery Trail
series to create this book.

Michael O. Perry, Author

Hal Calbom, Editor

Susan Perry Piper, Publisher

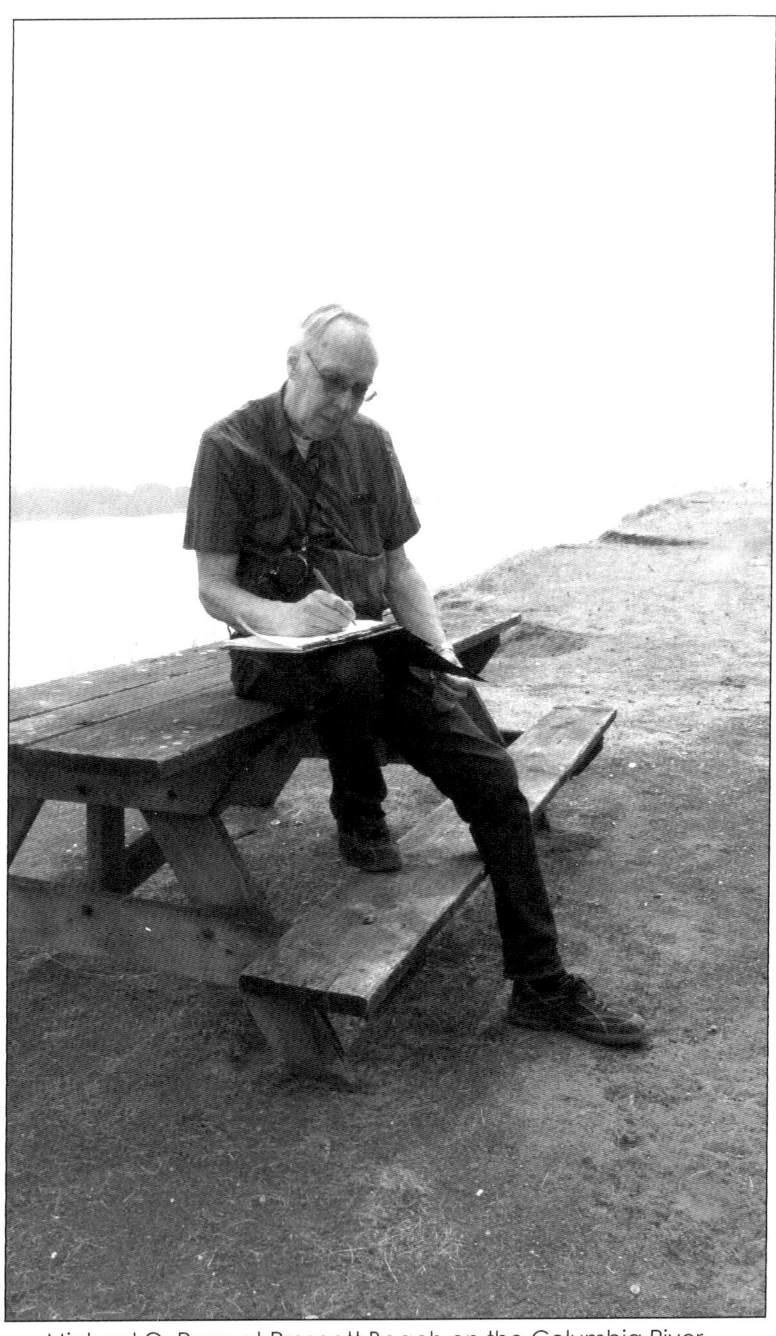

Michael O. Perry at Prescott Beach on the Columbia River

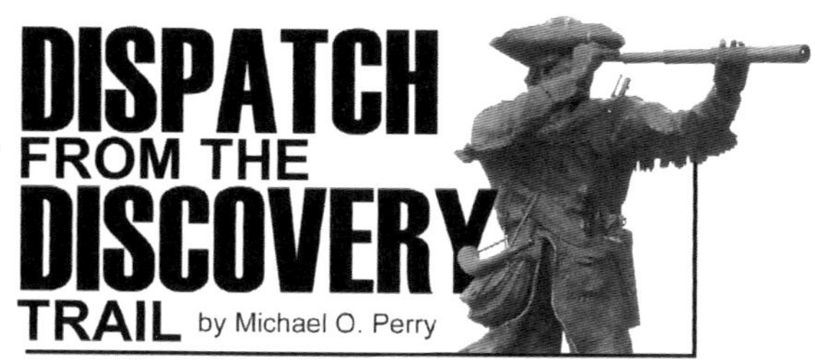

DISPATCH
FROM THE
DISCOVERY
TRAIL by Michael O. Perry

Publisher's Note:

When I bought the Columbia River Reader in early 2004 I had in mind to document the 29-month Lewis and Clark Expedition in conjunction with the planned Bicentennial Commemoration launching that April. I asked Michael O. Perry, about to retire as an environmental technician at Weyerhaeuser, if he had any interest in telling the story.

He did, and our readers loved it. We've since re-run the series twice by popular demand. Now, we have collected these dispatches in a single volume — annotated with Mike's further reflections and expanded with notes — in a page-to-page text and context format designed for easy reading and reference.

Michael has the eye of an artist, the curiosity of a scientist, and the Pacific Northwest in his heart. His layman's-eye-view illuminates key moments and invites our interest. The brilliant woodcuts of artist Debby Neely, another favorite and friend of Columbia River Reader Press, add a naturalist's sensibility to the narrative.

We hope you will enjoy this different way of seeing and experiencing the 8,000-mile Expedition with a new appreciation of its significance and accomplishment.

Susan P. Piper, Publisher

MICHAEL O. PERRY

dispatches

FROM THE DISCOVERY TRAIL

WITH HAL CALBOM

WOODCUT ART BY DEBBY NEELY

A LAYMAN'S LEWIS & CLARK

Dispatches from the Discovery Trail

by Michael O. Perry

PUBLISHED BY
Columbia River Reader Press
Longview, Washington
copyright MMXX
All rights reserved.

PRINTED
in the United State of America.

The scanning, uploading and distribution of this book via the Internet or via any other means without the permission of the publisher is illegal and punishable by law. Please purchase only authorized electronic editions, and do not participate in or encourage electronic piracy of copyrighted materials.

Your support of the author's rights is appreciated.

ISBN NUMBER: 978-1-7346725-4-1

For additional information or
to order additional copies:
Columbia River Reader Press
1333 14th Avenue
Longview, WA 98632
publisher@crreader.com

Design and Layout: Susan Piper
Editing, Notes, Interview: Hal Calbom

Woodcut art by Debby Neely
Cover and Inside Cover: "Whispering"
Frontispiece: "Heron"
Woodcuts listed by title, page 239.
Copyright Debby Neely and Columbia River Reader Press.

Quoted journal entries in italics are
Reprinted from "The Definitive Journals of Lewis and Clark,"
edited by Gary E. Moulton, by permission of the
University of Nebraska Press.

Reproductions from the authentic journals of
Lewis and Clark used with permission from the
American Philosophical Society.

"Dispatch from the Discovery Trail" originally appeared in
Columbia River Reader, April 2004 – February 2021.
All rights reserved.

www.crreader.com/crrpress

CONTENTS

CONTENTS

The author quotes extensively from the 13-volume "The Definitive Journals of Lewis and Clark," edited by Gary B. Moulton, and along with Columbia River Reader Press's editor and publisher, gratefully acknowledge the generosity of University of Nebraska Press and the kind assistance of Leif Milliken in arranging for their use in "Dispatches from the Discovery Trail."

THE

Vision

Editor's Note: The complete text of the original 33-episode Dispatch series, including sidebar material, appears on right-hand pages. This text is accompanied by new context and author commentary on the left-hand pages.

... deception of Congress ...

Jefferson described an expedition confined to the Mississippi River basin and purely for purposes of expanding commerce.

... the weakest claim ...

"The fact that Gray found the inlet of the river was a very important thing but he didn't explore the river. He didn't go upstream at all. He just stayed down there in the estuary. The British came in and went all the way up to Portland, basically, within a couple of years."

DISPATCHES FROM THE DISCOVERY TRAIL

"I knew that if I was going to write this, it had to be something that was going to be written for the common person like myself. When I first looked at all the books I thought, 'This is really dry, most of it. How do we get this to where it's going to be a monthly column in a newspaper?'" ~ *Michael O. Perry*

EPISODE 1

Why Our Founding Father Thomas Jefferson Lied to Congress

Modern day presidents aren't the only ones who conduct covert operations. Thomas Jefferson, author of the Declaration of Independence and our third president, helped define and ensure the American way of life.

Yet, if it hadn't been for his vision and strategy — and his deception of Congress when he sent Lewis and Clark to explore the western lands — those of us living in the Pacific Northwest today might be flying a different flag.

The weakest claim

Lewis and Clark often get credit for being the first white men to cross North America by land, but Canadians know that Alexander Mackenzie earned the honor. He was a member of the North West Company that competed with the Hudson Bay Company to dominate the fur trade in what is now the Pacific Northwest.

Mackenzie followed parts of the Peace and Fraser Rivers to the Pacific Ocean in 1793, publishing a full account of his explorations in 1801. A year later, Thomas Jefferson read Mackenzie's story.

While he undoubtedly admired Mackenzie's accomplishment, Jefferson also knew it strengthened Britain's claim to the Pacific Northwest. In addition to England, the Oregon Territory was also claimed by Spain, Russia and the United States — which had the weakest claim, based on Robert Gray's discovery of the mouth of the Columbia River in 1792.

Knowing he must act fast to protect America's interest, Jefferson aimed to strengthen his country's claim by launching an expedition to find the most direct water route to the Pacific Ocean.

At the time, two-thirds of the United States' population lived within 50 miles of the Atlantic Ocean and its tidewaters.

People living beyond the Appalachian Mountains felt isolated and many favored secession from the United States to form a separate country.

From sea to shining sea

However, Jefferson didn't see the mountains as a dividing line. He had long promoted exploring the lands west of the Mississippi River, with the idea of eventually making the United States reach from coast to coast.

Jefferson believed the massive Columbia River reached inland to the Rocky Mountains. He thought following the Missouri River to its headwaters and taking a short overland portage across the continental divide might lead to the headwaters of the Columbia River.

Sending an American expedition along that route would strengthen America's claim to the western half of North America. Such a trek, however, was not authorized by the Constitution and could be considered an armed intrusion into foreign lands — including the Indians'.

Satisfying curiosity

In early 1803, Congress approved the $2,500 Jefferson requested for an expedition promoting commerce, going no farther west than the Mississippi basin. However, Jefferson told his private secretary, Meriwether Lewis, that this official explanation "satisfied curiosity" and "masks sufficiently the real destination."

Congress didn't know it, but Jefferson had already made plans and picked Lewis to lead the expedition.

While the early Americans had been creating a new country along the east coast, France, Russia, England and Spain had laid claim to the western half of the continent. France ceded its claims to Spain in 1762, so Spain owned everything west of the Mississippi River except the Oregon Territory.

In 1800, Napoleon decided he wanted the land back, and Spain relented since it was no longer a world power. It took two years for word of that transfer to reach Jefferson and he was not pleased. A few months earlier, he had asked Spain's permission to travel up the Missouri in an effort to reach the Pacific coast, and they hadn't mentioned France was the new landlord. Spain did say its explorers had already shown conclusively there was no water route between the Missouri and the Pacific.

Jefferson let Napoleon know the United States would not tolerate French control of land in North America. Before

... Jefferson sent an envoy to Paris ...

“Their instructions were to buy New Orleans and as much of the land between there and Florida as they could. And when they get there, and Napoleon says, ‘I need some money to fight my war, we’ll sell you everything in North America for a few million...’ it was more than they were authorized to spend, but they knew a good deal.”

... is now Washington and Oregon ...

“Without the expedition there probably would have been a fight over this territory. Looking back at it, I say Spain had the longest, best claim to it of any of them. France had some fur trappers, and the English had all kinds of outposts and trading activity. Our only claims were Gray at the mouth and Lewis and Clark coming overland.”

resorting to war, Jefferson sent an envoy to Paris in 1803 to try to negotiate the purchase of New Orleans and as much of the Mississippi Valley as possible.

Meanwhile, Napoleon had his hands full with the resumption of the Anglo-French War, so he decided to cut his losses in America and raise some money to fight his war in Europe.

They knew a good deal

When France offered to sell all its holdings in North America for $15 million, the American envoy accepted although they had only been authorized to spend $10 million. They knew a good deal when they saw one.

The news reached Jefferson on July 4, 1803: America had doubled in size overnight!

Remember the story about a Dutch merchant buying Manhattan Island from the Indians in 1626 for $24 worth of beads? Well, the purchase of half the continent for three cents an acre was an even bigger steal.

The stage was set! Thanks to Jefferson's behind-the-scenes efforts, America was ready to send the Corps of Discovery westward to reinforce its claim to what would eventually become the western half of the United States. Without that expedition, it is likely England or Russia would have ended up with what is now Washington and Oregon.

What the Lewis and Clark Expedition set out to accomplish was similar in scope and magnitude to America's space exploration program. And while the actual trip on the Missouri River began on May 14, 1804, the expedition officially began a year earlier.

... To salute the Bicentennial ...

Lewis and Clark fell into relative obscurity during the rest of the 19th century. In the early 20th century, the Louisiana Purchase Exposition was organized in 1904 in St. Louis, Missouri. The following year, 1905, Portland, Oregon, held the Lewis and Clark Centennial Exposition, a feat of civic boosterism as much as historical recollection. Much of the memory of the Expedition over the years was kept alive using currency, U.S. postage stamps, the naming of U.S. naval vessels, geographic locations and a college, Lewis and Clark, in Portland.

TO SALUTE THE BICENTENNIAL of the Lewis and Clark Expedition, the U.S. Postal Service issued three attractive commemorative stamps in May 2004.

Two stamps featured individual portraits of Meriwether Lewis and William Clark painted by Michael J. Deas. These were only available in a 32-page Prestige booklet containing 10 each of the two stamps. The booklet featured informative text, historic illustrations and scenic photographs relating to the Corps of Discovery's exploration of the Louisiana Purchase during 1804-1806. The booklet had a limited distribution, available in just 10 cities, including Ilwaco, Washington, and Astoria, Oregon. This souvenir book, which originally sold for $8.95 ($1.55 over face value), is available on eBay for $10 or less and is worth owning.

A third stamp showed Lewis and Clark together on a mountain top. That stamp was available in sheets of 20 in all post offices in the United States.

All three stamps are still valid for postage. However, you will need to add additional postage to your letter since the first-class letter rate increases regularly.

EPISODE 2

WANTED: Stout, Healthy Unmarried Men

On May 14, 1804, the Corps of Discovery set out on a journey that would cover almost 8,000 miles and take more than two years to complete. Preparations for the trip began a year earlier.

While the Lewis and Clark Expedition was a bigger undertaking, it was similar to camping trips many families take every summer — loading up the SUV, driving to the end of the road and hiking into the backcountry for a week or two. If you forget something, a credit card comes in handy; if you get lost, there's always your cell phone.

But Lewis and Clark had to take everything they would need for the next two years. Their "camping" trip would take them into areas where no white man had ever set foot. They took items to trade with Indians for supplies. And while they would carry a letter of credit from President Jefferson, there were no stores or hotels along their route, and nobody knew if they would find a trading ship waiting when — or if — they reached the Pacific coast.

... to receive instruction ...

Besides Jefferson's impetus, the Expedition enjoyed the sponsorship of the American Philosophical Society, which strengthened its claim to be a journey of exploration and discovery, not simply a land grab. Lewis and Clark rewarded the Society for its hours of tutoring in natural science by cataloging more than 200 new plant and animal species during the Expedition.

... the United States now owned ...

"The Purchase now made it easier for them to get the money from Congress, because they're going to go out now and establish trade, not just discover and explore. Jefferson wanted to go out and establish trade relations with the Indians, and let them know that we're the new owner of the land, and to quit trading with the British and the French, because our people are coming out. Our business people will come out and set up trading posts."

During the spring and summer of 1803, Jefferson and Lewis worked feverishly to get organized. The President arranged for Lewis to receive instruction from prominent American scientists about botany, natural history, mineralogy and astronomy. Jefferson also secured passports from the French and British governments to allow the expedition to cross their territory.

However, the President's most important contribution was his detailed instructions on June 20, 1803. I can only imagine today's English teachers cringing at Jefferson's run-on sentences in the following excerpts from his letter to Lewis:

The object of your mission is to explore the Missouri river, & such principal streams of it, as, by it's course and communication with the waters of the Pacific ocean, whether the Columbia, Oregon, Colorado or any other river may offer the most direct and practicable water communication across this continent for the purposes of commerce.

Beginning at the mouth of the Missouri, you will take observations of latitude & longitude, at all remarkeable points on the river, & expecially at the mouths of rivers. Your observations are to be taken with great pains & accuracy. Several copies of these as well as your other notes should be made at leisure times, & put into the care of the most trust-worthy of your attendants, to guard, by multiplying them, against the accidental losses to which they will be exposed.

Jefferson clearly valued the lives of the expedition members, but he valued even more the information that would be lost if they died en route.

He told Lewis to turn back if the journey proved too dangerous. If they reached the Pacific coast, Jefferson wanted Lewis to send copies of all the notes and maps back by ship, if possible. He didn't want to risk the loss of everything on a return trip by land.

Lewis was also to serve as Jefferson's roving ambassador to the Indian nations they encountered. He was told to collect as much information as possible about each tribe's territorial boundaries, their numbers, cultures, languages, religions, clothing, customs and housing.

Lewis was instructed to be friendly to all Indians, unless circumstances prevented it, and to inform them the United States now owned the Louisiana Territory. However, none of these instructions were to interfere with the principal goal: finding a practical water route to the Pacific.

So what kind of supplies did Lewis take? Obviously, surveying equipment and blank journals for record keeping. Just as

... lots of whiskey...

"I mean, you think about 300 gallons, and 30 people. And every day, they were given a gill of whiskey. How much is a gill? Four ounces."

important were the guns and ammunition needed for both hunting and protection. Lewis expected the men would be able to feed and clothe themselves by hunting along the route.

While they took little food, they made room for lots of whiskey, a standard military ration in those days. They took tools such as axes, drills, and files. They also took a hundred pounds of "Indian presents" (beads, fishhooks, cloth, needles and knives) and a wide assortment of medicines.

Guns were obtained from the federal arsenal at Harper's Ferry, Virginia. One of the guns was an air rifle, which was to be of great interest to the Indians along the way. Lewis also had a 40-foot long collapsible iron-framed canoe made at Harper's Ferry. The ribbed frame could be folded up until needed, and then covered with animal hides or bark. It sounded like a good idea, but Lewis would be disappointed when it failed to live up to expectations.

In a June 19, 1803 letter to William Clark, Lewis said he wanted "stout, healthy, unmarried men, accustomed to the woods, and capable of bearing bodily fatigue in a pretty considerable degree." Most men were recommended by their army commanders, and about 45 men gathered at Camp Dubois near the junction of the Missouri and Mississippi Rivers to spend the winter of 1803 getting ready to start their epic journey the next spring.

Next episode, we will retrace the steps of the Corps of Discovery as they made their way up the Missouri River.

"LEWIS AND CLARK,"1804 © BY L. EDWARD FISHER AND COMMISSIONED BY THE MISSOURI BANKERS ASSOCIATION

This painting commemorates the two pirogues and 55-foot keelboat used by the Corps of Discovery, perhaps the best moment the keelboat ever enjoyed. It was a continuous source of blood, sweat and tears as the Expedition worked its way up the Missouri.

... disciplinary problems ...

"This is hard for us to comprehend today. But it reminds us this was a military expedition, which might have been key to their survival. I could see this happening once, but these same guys were court martialed again later for stealing whiskey and get lashed again. I mean, 50 lashes. And the Indians were appalled when they saw that. They just could not believe that anybody was that cruel."

EPISODE 3

Rewards and Punishments of a Rigorous Trip

How would you convince 45 young men to join a two-year expedition into the unknown? The promise of free land and a paycheck made many men eager to sign up, but Lewis and Clark were concerned desertions might be a problem later, when the going got tough. As an extra perk, they took about 300 gallons of whiskey. By the time the "bar" ran dry a year later, the explorers would be too far from civilization for anyone to risk leaving.

Every night, each man got a gill (a quarter-pint) of whiskey — enough to ease the rigors of the day and, by today's standards, make him legally drunk.

This is why they didn't backpack

When the Corps of Discovery departed from the location of present-day St. Louis Gateway Arch, they were a party, but a sober one. The group left at 4 pm on May 14, 1804, *"under a jentle brease"* and progressed only four miles up the Missouri River that day. The 55-foot keelboat, carrying 12 tons of supplies and 25 men, could be rowed, sailed, pushed, or pulled. Two pirogues (flat-bottomed dugout canoes) and four horses carried the additional supplies.

While most men were members of the U.S. military, French Canadians were hired as interpreters and to help get the heavily-laden boats up the mighty Missouri. It is unknown exactly how many men began the journey.

Captain Clark was in charge the first week, since Captain Lewis was still in St. Louis procuring supplies. In reality, "Captain" Clark was only a Lieutenant. The Army had refused to assign him the rank of Captain as Lewis had promised. So, for the entire journey, Lewis treated Clark as a co-Captain and the men never knew the difference.

Just three days into the journey, disciplinary problems arose. Three men sneaked away from camp to get some whiskey. When they returned, they were court martialed by a jury of their peers. One man received 50 lashes across his bare back with a cat-o'-nine-tails. This punishment was harsh but not unusual. In the six months it took to reach North Dakota, five courts-martial would be held to hear nine cases involving six members of the crew.

These displays are part of a permanent exhibit at the Columbia Gorge Discovery Center and Museum at The Dalles, Oregon.

… 33 tons …

To emphasize the sheer weight and mass of the supplies carried when they embarked, a Bicentennial exhibit amassed canisters and cargo representing 33 tons. Above are replicas of 52 lead canisters, each containing four pounds of gun powder and eight pounds of lead, devised by Lewis. Once emptied, each canister was melted down to make lead bullets in a mold. In addition, 33 metal canisters were made to hold 193 pounds of "portable soup."

Stuck in the mud, again

The keelboat was so heavily loaded that it often became stuck on sandbars or snags, sometimes requiring the off-loading of enough supplies to re-float the boat. An event described in Clark's May 24th journal entry was to be repeated many times:

"The swiftness of the Current wheeled the boat, Broke our Toe rope, and was nearly over Setting the boat, all hand Jumped out on the upper Side and bore on that Side until the Sand washed from under the boat..." Part of the problem was the way supplies were loaded: *"The barge ran foul... several times on logs... this was ca[u]sed by her being too heavily laden in the stern."*

Not all of the men rode in boats; some walked along the riverbank and hunted for food. Records indicate they carried 30 tons of supplies, including a ton of whiskey and seven tons of parched corn, meal, flour, pork, and other food — enough to last just 45 days. Thus, hunting for bear, deer and birds was very important.

A week into the trip, they traded two quarts of whiskey to some Kickapoo Indians for a pheasant and four deer. By the middle of June, two-thirds of the men had scurvy. They were eating practically nothing but meat and no fresh fruit or vegetables. The men consumed up to ten pounds of meat per day just to resupply the calories burned.

The going was slow against the strong current in the lower Missouri, with progress averaging only about 1.5 miles per hour (a leisurely walking pace is 2mph). The work was extraordinarily hard: *"I observe that the men Swet more than is common from Some cause, I think the Missouri's Water is the principal Cause... the Sweet pores off the men in Streams..."* A day spent walking along the river hunting was a welcome relief from the drudgery of rowing, poling, or pulling the boats upstream.

Food: A constant problem

Days would pass without the hunters killing anything. But as they went upriver, they began to find different varieties of fruits and berries:

"a butifull bottom Plain of about 2000 acres covered with wild rye & Potatoes intermix't with the grass... wild rice was plenty groeing on the bank of the River, Strawberyes..." and *"The Praries Come within a Short distance of the river on each Side which Contains in addition to Plumbs Raspberries & vast quantities of wild apples... great numbs. of Deer are seen feeding on the young willows & earbage in the Banks and on the Sand bars in the river."*

... Musquetors ...

"William Clark's spelling has amused and amazed people over the years. I didn't go through and verify them all, but the story is that he spelled the word 'mosquito" either 26 or 32 different ways during his journaling, and never got it right. It helps to remember they had no dictionaries on the trip. It's amazing some of the spellings are as uniform as they are."

As the Expedition progressed up the Missouri, they met several fur traders returning with a load of pelts. Whenever time allowed, they would stop to talk to boats coming downstream, hoping to learn more about what to expect upstream. Although they started out between 5–7am each morning, only 10–15 miles was covered each day. After a month, they had traveled only 250 miles. It rained much of the first month, leading to journal entries like *"The Ticks & Musquetors are verry troublesome."* They purchased 300 pounds of buffalo grease (or bear lard?) and tallow from a French fur trader to be used as insect repellent.

On June 14, a crew member reported an amazing encounter that Clark recorded: *"he heard in this Pond a Snake making goubleing noises like a turkey, he fired his gun & the noise was increased…& may be herd Several miles, This Snake is of emence size."* Maybe that man received an extra ration of whiskey the night before?

By June 26, the Expedition had covered 400 miles, reaching what is now Kansas. On June 29, two more courts-martial were held. The previous night, the sentry in charge of guarding the whiskey helped himself to an extra ration (or two or three), resulting in his becoming very drunk. Another soldier came along and helped himself to the whiskey, too. These were the same men court martialed on May 17. The next morning, other crew members were very upset to learn what happened. After all, it was the crew's whiskey that the two men had been drinking. The sentry was sentenced to 100 lashes and his cohort got 50, administered by their crew mates. As Clark wrote, *"we have always found the men verry ready to punish Such crimes."*

Marked with a bang!

The crew celebrated Independence Day by firing the bow cannon on the keel boat in the morning and then *"closed the* [day] *by a Discharge from our bow piece, an extra Gill of whiskey."*

On July 11, one of the two guards fell asleep on his post. This was one of the most serious offenses that could be committed, punishable by death. The poor soul may have preferred death; his sentence was 100 lashes — 25 lashes a day for each of the next four days. While it is hard to imagine such brutal punishment, it isn't hard to imagine what might have happened if a roving band of Sioux had come upon the camp while the guard was asleep.

Next episode we will continue our trip up the Missouri River and learn of the only Corps of Discovery member to die on the Expedition.

THE

River

... unknown territory ...

"There's a good reason we don't hear much of significance, really, about the entire first year of the Expedition. When they were going up the Missouri from St. Louis to Fort Mandan, they're doing virtually nothing but working their butts off every day going against the current, and moving their keelboat off sand bars and through logs and brush. The territory was already explored and known."

EPISODE 4

Peace Pipes, Pills and Birthdays in the "Garden of Eden"

When the Expedition departed St. Louis in 1804, it was questionable whether members of the Corps of Discovery would survive their daring and dangerous quest into the unknown. But despite lack of medical care, poor diet and miserable conditions, only one crew member died on the trip.

Medical care had been of great concern to Lewis and Clark. Before starting the journey, Lewis studied medical treatments and procedures. He took along about 30 different pills and drugs to be administered as needed. Still, medical knowledge 200 years ago was not what it is today, and most remedies are laughed at now.

Dr. Benjamin Rush, a top physician of the day, sent along 50 dozen purging pills with Lewis and Clark. These pills, containing a mixture of mercury, chlorine and dried morning glory root, were thought to be a cure for pretty much all the ills of mankind and were the medicine of choice for almost every ailment. They were, however, undoubtedly the wrong thing to use in most cases. The pills were a strong purgative of explosive power and the results so awesome they were called Rush's "Thunderbolts," or "Thunderclappers."

Very few of Lewis and Clark's campsites can be accurately located today, but modern-day researchers have managed to identify some by the mercury content of soil in former latrine sites.

On July 7th the journals tell of *"one man verry Sick, Struck with the sun, Capt. Lewis bled him & gave Niter which has revived him much."* Bleeding was a standard remedy of the time, and potassium nitrate (saltpeter) was used to increase the flow of urine and perspiration.

Mosquitoes and gnats continued to be a major problem. Some mosquitoes probably carried malaria. Clark made numerous entries in his journal about the pesky insects. In fact, he spelled the word mosquito 26 different ways (*musqutors, musquetors, musquitors, mosquitors, misqutors, misquitors, etc.*) and never once got it right!

The Lewis and Clark Expedition officially started on May 14, 1804, but the men would not begin exploring unknown territory until 1805. Fur trappers and Indian traders had previously explored and mapped the Missouri River from St. Louis up to present-day Bismark, North Dakota. But there was still a great sense of discovery as the Corps members documented new species of animals and plant varieties in the journals.

… light my fire …

"We hear so much about food eaten and cooked, and I always wondered something more basic — how did they light all these fires when half the time, especially on the Pacific Coast, they are drenched by rain all day and firewood was scarce? I attended a re-enactment at Fort Clatsop while researching the series and found out about "char cloth," and a guy there, a re-enactor, showed me how they did it. He gets some moss and if you let the wind blow through it it dries quickly. Then he takes a chunk of cedar and takes a knife and starts whittling off little shavings — and the wind keeps drying stuff out.

And then they take out their little magic silver pill bottle, like a little round thing you keep your pills in, and there is this piece of char cloth. I said, 'Char cloth, what is char cloth?' He says it's a piece of cotton that they fold up, put in the little tin and stick it in the fire. It's got a hole in it, one little hole on top for air to get in. It gets hot and there's enough oxygen in there that it starts to burn but then it can't burn anymore and that cotton turns to charcoal, basically. So, when they need to light a fire they take the char cloth out and put it down there in their little bird's nest and they take a couple pieces of flint — chip, chip, chip, make sparks and pretty quickly that char cloth catches fire."

On July 29, a French fur trapper was sent to invite Oto and Missouri Indian chiefs to come to a council (near present-day Council Bluffs, Iowa). When he hadn't returned after four days, it became obvious he had either run into trouble or deserted. A day later, a regular member of the expedition disappeared. Detachments went out to look for both men.

Pink slip

They did not locate the elusive Frenchman, but after two weeks of searching, they found the Corps member and brought him back to face charges of desertion, a crime serious enough to warrant hanging or a firing squad. Instead, he was court-martialed and received a flogging and dishonorable discharge. He ran the gauntlet four times, with each member of the Corps striking him with nine switches as he went by. Indians present were dismayed by the harsh punishment and asked for mercy. While the deserter was expelled from the Corps, he stayed with the party until the spring of 1805 when the keelboat was sent back to St. Louis.

Why can't we be friends?

Six Oto and Missouri Indian chiefs and some warriors arrived at camp on August 2. Clark *"Sent them Som rosted meat Pork flour & meal, in return they Sent us Water millions."* At a council held the next day, the captains put on their full dress uniforms, raised the American flag, and paraded the men to create a ceremonial atmosphere. They delivered a long speech telling the Indians they had a new "great father" (Thomas Jefferson), that Americans wanted the Indians to trade exclusively with them and to stop warring with other Indian tribes.

The Indians wanted guns to wage war with the Teton Sioux, who were fast becoming the dominant power in the area. While neither side got what they wanted, a calumet (a ceremonial native pipe) was smoked and presents exchanged. The chiefs received peace medals with Jefferson's profile on the front and two clasped hands on the back.

Dinner on the hoof

The Great Plains was a Garden of Eden that no American had ever seen. Herds of elk numbered in the thousands, buffalo herds stretched as far as the eye could see, and deer appeared as plentiful as chickens on a farm. Clark turned 34 on August 1, and his dinner menu demonstrates the diversity of food available from the land now known as our nation's breadbasket: *"This being my birth day I order'd a Saddle of fat Vennison, an Elk fleece & a Bevertail to be cooked and a Desert of Cherries, Plumbs, Raspberries, Currents and grapes of a Supr. Quality."* Besides those fruits and berries, Clark noted *"the Praries Contain* (crab) *Apple, Gooseberris and Hastlenuts and a great Variety of Plants & flours not Common to the U S. What a field for a Betents* [botanist] *and a natirless"* [naturalist].

... The Peace Nickel series ...

The back of this U.S. Nickel created in 2004 features the design from the Peace Medal Lewis and Clark gave to Indians they met on their journey. The design shows two hands clasped in friendship: the military uniform cuff symbolized the United States, and the eagle-engraved wristband represents Native Americans with whom the U.S. wished to forge good relations. Above the hands, a crossed peace pipe and tomahawk symbolize peace. Three additional nickels were introduced showing Lewis and Clark's keelboat, the American bison, and a scene depicting 'Ocian in View! O! the Joy,' with Thomas Jefferson's likeness on the other side.

When Captain Lewis celebrated his 30th birthday on August 18th *"the evening was Closed with an extra Gill of Whiskey & a Dance until 11 oClock."* One of the men who had brought along his fiddle played it that night when the men gathered around the campfire.

Only one man died

Disaster struck less than 100 days into the journey. Sgt. Charles Floyd became very sick on August 19 with *"Beliose Chorlick,"* and was nursed through the night by Captain Clark. The next morning, while Clark was preparing a warm bath *"hopeing it would brace him a little"* Floyd died, most likely from appendicitis. Even if he had been in Philadelphia, likely nothing could have helped him — not even Dr. Rush's Thunderclappers. Floyd was buried on the top of a bluff in Iowa.

Next episode we will learn about prairie dogs and the crew's efforts to capture one, and the discovery of dinosaur bones.

... they only caught one of them ...

Spending most of September 7, 1804, digging and flooding their tunnels, the crew managed to catch just one prairie dog. Lewis had a cage built for it with the intention of shipping it back to Washington D.C. for President Jefferson to see firsthand. Lewis loaded the caged prairie dog onto the keelboat and fed it every day in an effort to keep it alive. The crew would continue up the Missouri until the end of October when they reached the Mandan Indian villages near present day Bismarck, North Dakota.

Seven months after it was captured, the live prairie dog was loaded onto the keelboat, along with various plant and animal specimens, for the trip back to St. Louis. While it took more than five months to travel from St. Louis up to the Mandan villages, the return trip took just a month and a half. From St. Louis, the cargo was put on another boat and sent down the Mississippi River to New Orleans. Another ship took the cargo through the Gulf of Mexico, around Florida, and up the coast to Baltimore.

In August 1805 (almost a year after it was captured), the prairie dog arrived in Washington, D.C., alive! However, Jefferson was still at Monticello, and did not arrive in Washington until October 4, 1805. Jefferson then shipped the prairie dog to a natural history museum in Philadelphia, where it lived until at least April 5, 1806. No mere barking squirrel, he.

EPISODE 5

A Dinosaur, Plesiosaur and Prairie Dogs

How would *you* go about capturing a prairie dog to send to the President of the United States? And why would you want to do it in the first place? Many readers who have tried to catch a mole in their lawn or garden will get a kick out of what Lewis and Clark did.

By August 1804, Lewis and Clark's Corp of Discovery had made their way up the Missouri River to present day South Dakota. While French trappers had been in the area for at least 75 years, the Corps of Discovery members were the first Americans to see the vast expanse of the Great Plains, which was a virtual Garden of Eden.

Every time they saw a new animal, they shot at least one so Lewis or Clark could make the detailed examination needed to fulfill Thomas Jefferson's instructions to document unknown plants and wildlife they encountered.

In the first four months of their journey, they had seen many new species of animals, including the coyote, magpie, gray wolf, mule deer, pronghorn (often wrongly called an antelope), and prairie dog.

Prairie dogs fascinated Lewis and Clark, and they saw a staggering number.

Some biologists believe there were 5 billion prairie dogs at that time, while 200 years later they were candidates for protection under the Endangered Species Act. As late as 1905, a government scientist found a village covering an area the size of West Virginia and housing an estimated 400 million prairie dogs!

Flush them out!

Lewis was so intrigued by the prairie dog that he decided to catch a live specimen to ship to Washington, D.C. Clark wrote "*near the foot of this high Nole we discovered a Village of an annamale... which burrow in the grown. The Village of those little dogs is under the ground a considerable distance. We dig under 6 feet thro rich hard clay without getting to their Lodges.*"

Patrick Gass reported "*Captain Lewis and Captain Clarke with all the party... took with them all the kettles and other vessels for holding water in order to drive the animals out of their holes by pouring in water; but though they worked at the business till night they only caught one of them.*"

According to Clark, "*Some of their wholes we put in 5 barrels of water without driving them out, we caught one by the water forceing him out. The Village of those animals Covs. about 4 acrs of Ground on a Gradual decent of a hill and Contains great numbers of holes on the top of which those little animals Set erect make a Whistling noise and whin alarmed Slip into their hole.*

A bit of arsenic ought to do it

Earlier, Clark had written of a close call Lewis experienced:"*by examination this Bluff Contained Alum, Copperas, Cobalt, Pyrites; a Alum Rock Soft & Sand Stone... also a clear Soft Substance which... I believe to be arsenic. Capt. Lewis in proveing the quality of those minerals was Near poisoning himself by the fumes & tast of the Cobalt which had the appearance of Soft Isonglass. Copperas & alum is very pisen, Capt. Lewis took a Dost of Salts to work off the effects of the arsenic.*" Three days later, Lewis was still suffering: "*Capt. Lewis much fatigued from heat the day it being verry hot & he being in a debilitated State from the Precautions he was obliged to take to prevent the effects of the Cobalt, & Minl Substance which had like to have poisoned him two days ago*" Maybe he had added insult to injury by taking some of Dr. Rush's Thunderclapper pills that consisted of a mixture of mercury and chlorine?

Two days after Lewis tried to poison himself, the expedition came upon an area the Indians were deathly afraid to go near. Clark called it Spirit Mound and wrote "*in an imence Plain a high Hill is Situated, and appears of a Conic form and by the different nations of Indians in this quarter is Suppose to be the residence of Deavels, that they are in human form with remarkable large heads and about 18 Inches high, that they are Very watchfull, and are arm'd with Sharp arrows with which they Can Kill at a great distance; they are Said to Kill all persons who are So hardy as to attempt to approach the hill; they State that tradition informs them that many Indians have Suffered by those little people and among others three Mahar men fell a Sacrefise to their murceyless fury not many years Since – so much do the Mahas Souix Ottoes and other neibhbouring nations believe this fable that no consideration is suffecient to induce them to approach the hill.*"

One of the maps they obtained in St. Louis told of a volcano in South Dakota, but they were unable to locate it. Possibly it was a burning seam of coal (lignite) a St. Louis trader had seen.

One thing they did find was a dinosaur. In 1804, nobody even knew about dinosaurs (the word wasn't coined until 1845). But, in present day South Dakota, Clark found fossil remains of a plesiosaur, an ocean-dwelling creature of the Mesozoic Era. Clark wrote "*we found a back bone with most of the entire laying Connected for 45 feet, those bones are petrified, Some teeth & ribs also Connected.*" Some of the vertebra are now in the Smithsonian Museum.

... a dinosaur ...

"*Nobody at all seemed even to know what dinosaurs were at this date. They obviously didn't know what they had found, but it's hard to believe that somebody hadn't found big bones before somewhere, but I don't know if they had. So, the option was just leave it, or put it on the trusty keelboat. And here are these poor guys that have been pulling that beast — the keelboat, not the dinosaur — and pushing and sweating upstream, and they say, 'here you go, here's a couple hundred more pounds of bones for you.'*"

Loopy over the froot

The richness of the Great Plains was most impressive. As Clark wrote earlier, "*The Plains of this countrey are covered with a Leek Green Grass, well calculated for the sweetest and most norushing hay – interspersed with Cops of trees, Spreding ther lofty branchs over Pools Springs or Brooks of fine water. Groops of Shrubs covered with the most delicious froot is to be seen in every direction, and nature appears to have exerted herself to butify the Senery by the variety of flours Delicately and highly flavered raised above the Grass, which Strikes & profumes the Sensation, and amuses the mind throws it into Conjecturing the cause of So magnificient a Senery… in a Country thus Situated far removed from the Sivilised world.*"

Almost all of the native grassland has now been destroyed by farming. But along with the once uncountable buffalo and prairie dogs, there are still a few places left for people to see the same things Lewis and Clark's party saw. The same holds true for the Missouri River; with the exception of a short stretch of river in the southeast corner of South Dakota that is still free flowing, it is now just a series of lakes behind the many dams between St. Louis and Montana.

While some folks would like to preserve *everything* forever (including the Northwest forests), we should be thankful somebody saved at least a portion of it for future generations to enjoy.

Next episode we will learn of the tense meeting with the Teton Sioux, by far the most feared Indians in the west. Winter is fast approaching as they reach North Dakota.

... the weather was changing ...

"The going had been slow, but they'd been in what Clark called The Garden of Eden, rich American grasslands full of game and forage. Suddenly, as the fall approached, the members began to worry about three things: the Indians — chiefly the fierce Teton Sioux they'd heard warnings about — the weather, and the availability of game for food."

EPISODE 6

Bluffs and Bluster and Winter Weather Worries

Not all members of the Corp of Discovery were great hunters. George Shannon came close to starving to death when he got lost at the end of August in 1804 while looking for missing horses. In his attempt to return to the boats, Shannon followed an Indian trail; he thought he was behind the party, but he was actually ahead of them. After two weeks, he decided he was never going to catch up with the Expedition and stopped.

On Sept. 11th, his crewmates found him sitting on the riverbank, hoping to catch a ride back to St. Louis with a French trapper. Shannon must have been a poor marksman, for Clark wrote "*thus a man had the like to have Starved to death in a land of Plenty for the want of Bullitts.*" Shannon had gone "*12 days without any thing to eate but Grapes & one Rabit, which he Killed by shooting a piece of hard Stick in place of a ball.*"

Lewis and Clark had no way of knowing what lay ahead when the Expedition traveled through what is now South Dakota. But, worries about the approaching winter weather and interactions with the Indians were undoubtedly on their mind. Some of you may have driven across the Dakotas and feared being caught by a winter storm. Today, with reliable weather forecasts and motels along the way, few people actually get stranded. But, for Lewis and Clark, it was a real possibility.

On September 15, 1804, Clark wrote "*this evening is verry Cold... the wind is hard from the N W.*" Three days later, Lewis wrote "*this day saw the first brandt on their return from the north.*" Birds flying south was not a welcome sight since they were hoping to get to the Mandan Indian villages in present day North Dakota before winter snows set in.

The weather was changing. On September 23rd Clark wrote "*aire remarkably dry – in 36 hours two Spoonfuls of water aveporated in a sauser.*" On September 19th, they began recording temperatures each morning and again at 4pm each day. Over the next month, morning temperatures ranged from 38 to 58 degrees, and the afternoon highs ranged between 40 and 86. By mid-October, Clark wrote "*the leaves of all the trees as ash, elm &c except the cottonwood is now fallen.*" The men awoke to frost on the ground several times in early October. Clearly, winter was near.

Meanwhile, Lewis and Clark were worried about the Teton Sioux Indians. They knew a Teton war party had recently raided the Omahas, killing more than 70 people and capturing dozens more as slaves.

... make friends with the Teton Sioux ...

"These were the most aggressive Indians they'd run into yet. But they'd been warned , both parties. Everywhere the Expedition went, the Indians knew they were coming because other Indians passed the word. The fur trappers had told the Expedition members they should anticipate trouble getting by and might have to pay the Indians."

Sioux Chief Running Antelope is the only American Indian ever depicted on U.S. currency. Unfortunately, the Chief is pictured — to the distress of many historians and tribal leaders — wearing a Pawnee headdress, as his traditional Sioux headdress was too tall for the engraving.

The Teton Sioux were a large and aggressive tribe who controlled the land on both sides of the river and had prevented small groups of traders from passing without paying tribute. Lewis and Clark knew they had to deal with them since the Omaha survivors reported the Teton Sioux intended to prevent the Expedition from continuing up the river. President Jefferson had specifically instructed Lewis to make friends with the Teton Sioux; however, if Lewis recalled that order, he ignored it.

September 24th was the first of several tense days. First, the Teton Sioux stole the Expedition's last horse. Efforts to get the horse back failed when three chiefs met with Lewis and Clark to hear the standard speech promoting peace and trading. Unimpressed by the medals and presents they received, the chiefs were invited aboard the keelboat for some whiskey. The chiefs were *"exceedingly fond of it, they took up an empty bottle, Smelted it, and made many Simple jestures and Soon began to be troublesome."*

The chiefs resisted efforts to be put ashore; when a warrior grabbed the line holding the pirogue and one of the chiefs demanded a canoe load of presents before allowing the expedition to go on, Clark drew his sword and Lewis called all the men to arms. The swivel cannon was aimed at shore and the men loaded their rifles. The Indians strung their bows and took arrows from their quivers. Lewis held a lighted taper over the cannon and refused to back down. Disaster was averted when the warriors began to back off. Clark offered to shake hands with the few who remained, but they refused. Two of the three chiefs stepped forward and offered to stay on the keelboat that night to insure peace. The next morning, they asked Lewis to stay another night.

That evening, the Teton Sioux put on a grand pageant and feast. A scalp dance was performed (the scalps were from a recent raid against the neighboring Omaha Indians). Clark described it as "A *large fire made in the Center, about 10 misitions playing on tamberins made of hoops & skin stretched, long sticks with Deer & Goats Hoofs tied So as to make a gingling noise and many others of a similar kind, those men began to Sing & Beet on the Tamboren, the women Came forward highly Deckerated in their way, with the Scalps an Trofies of war of ther father Husbands Brothers or near Connection & proceeded to Dance the war Dance."*

While returning from the pageant, Clark's pirogue crashed into the keelboat and broke its anchor line. Clark ordered *"all hands up & at their ores"* to keep the loose boat from slipping into the swift current. The Indians became alarmed by the commotion and thought they were being attacked.

In no time, there were 200 warriors lined up on the bank, while the men on board had their guns loaded and aimed. Interestingly, as was the case the previous day, the Indians did not notch their

... fearless and prepared to fight ...

The Teton Sioux occupied two villages near present-day Pierre, South Dakota. Among French and Canadian traders, as well as among other neighboring and competing tribes, the Tetons were known for their fighting spirit and aggressiveness. They often demanded gifts or tribute for passage up or down the river.

At the first council with the leaders of the Teton tribe, the Expedition's leaders went through their regular routine used when meeting Indians, dressing in their parade uniforms and demonstrating their weapons. The Tetons were notably unimpressed. They saw the Americans as potential trade rivals and grew fractious as their council meetings went on. During the Corps' stay, Clark made detailed notes on Teton culture. In his journal, the Tetons are described as thin, small and generally ill-looking. The Teton men wore hawk feathers about their heads and robes over their bodies, while women dressed in buffalo skins and robes. During the Expedition's stay, the Tetons held a number of celebrations — scalp dances — of a recent war victory over the rival Omahas.

arrows – doing so might have been enough to cause the crew to begin shooting. The confusion was soon resolved. Clark wrote "*All prepared on board for any thing which might happen, we kept a Strong guard all night in the boat. No sleep.*"

When the crew attempted to leave the next morning, the Indians once again created a tense showdown. They demanded some more tobacco before allowing the expedition to proceed. Lewis lost his temper and refused. As they tried to cast off, a warrior grabbed the rope. Clark was not ready to repeat the previous standoffs, so he threw some tobacco to the chief while lighting the cannon's firing taper to show he was prepared to shoot if necessary. A few more pieces of tobacco and the confrontation was over and they were once again moving up river.

Although the Indians vastly outnumbered the expeditionary force, many would have been killed if fighting had occurred. Such a loss was too big a price to pay even for control of trade and travel on the river. Indians would not attack a well-armed and determined force. The French and Spanish traders who had preceded Lewis and Clark had been willing to pay whatever price the Indians demanded and were thus deemed to be weak.

Knowing the Corps clearly was fearless and prepared to fight, the Teton Sioux were not willing to fight when their bluffs and bluster failed. Lewis and Clark were fortunate since the entire crew would almost certainly have been killed if fighting had broken out. Such a victory would have made the Teton Sioux even more feared and would undoubtedly have changed history. The United States could not have sent trading parties up the river for years afterwards, and the westward expansion would have been slowed.

On October 8th, the expedition reached the Arikara Nation in present-day South Dakota. Word of the Corp's near-disasterous encounter with the Teton Sioux had already reached the Arikaras.

Things went much better when the two sides met, and Lewis gave them gifts. As usual, the keelboat cannon was fired to impress the Indians, and Lewis "*astonished them much*" when he fired his air rifle. But, the Indians were even more amazed by one of the men in the Expedition.

Next episode we will learn about the only Black man in the Corps of Discovery, and encounter the first snow as the Corps travels to the Mandan village in North Dakota where the group will spend the winter.

"YORK," BY CHARLES M. RUSSELL

Charles M. Russell

Montana's famed "cowboy artist" was fascinated by the Lewis and Clark Expedition. Having grown up in St. Louis, he witnessed the continuous embarkation of traders, trappers and explorers up the Missouri and listened to their exploits and tales. His painting of York and the Hidatsas meeting at Fort Mandan depicts the Hidatsa chief Le Borgne putting spit on his finger and attempting to rub the black away, believing it was only painted on. With his grand sense of the dramatic, Russell can be accused of romanticizing the west and the Native Americans. On the other hand, he was among the first to give the Indians primacy in many of his narrative works. Near the end of his career, Russell wrote, in 1914, *"This is the onley real American. He faught an died for his country. To day he has no vote, no country, and is not a citizen but history will not forget him."*

EPISODE 7

Heading for South Dakota

York: The Big Medison

Charles M. Russell's 1908 watercolor titled "York" depicts a March 1805 event, when a Hidatsa chief spit on his finger and tried to rub the black color off Clark's slave, York, but to no avail.

York, about 30, was a big, very dark, strong, agile man who had been Clark's lifelong companion from childhood. Although he was a slave, York was treated as a full member of the expedition.

Throughout their journey, Indians were fascinated by York and thought he was "the big Medison." Plains Indians frequently shared their wives with strangers possessing wealth or power they didn't have.

While Expedition journals make no mention of York's sexual activities, the 1814 narrative edition, prepared by Nicholas Biddle from the original journals, included additional information based on discussions with Captain Clark.

Biddle's account tells of a warrior who invited York to spend the night with his wife. The warrior stood guard at the door to prevent any interruptions, believing some of York's power would be transferred to himself through his wife.

Last month, this column found the Corps of Discovery looking for a place to spend the winter. After their tense confrontation with the aggressive Teton Sioux in late September 1804, they were anxious to be on their way. The men had covered 1,300 miles in the previous six months — an average of just seven miles per day. While they hoped to get further up the Missouri, they had underestimated the challenge of the rapidly flowing river. So the Corps decided to try to make it to the Mandan Indian villages in present-day North Dakota if possible.

The expedition reached the Arikara Nation in present-day South Dakota on October 8th. Things went much better than when the Corps had met with the Teton Sioux two weeks earlier. As usual, the keelboat cannon was fired to impress the Arikaras, and Lewis also fired his air rifle that "*astonished them much.*" But the Indians were even more amazed by one of the men in the expedition; Captain Clark had brought his slave, York, along. "*Those Indians wer much astonished at my servent, They never Saw a black man before, all flocked around him & examined him from top to toe... he made him Self more terrible in their view than I would have wished him to Doe... telling them that before I cought him he was wild & lived upon people, young children was verry good eating. Showed them his Strength &c. &c.*"

"A Bird's Eye View of the Mandan Village," by George Catlin

1,800 miles above St. Louis, 30 years after Lewis & Clark visited.

... the second Mandan village ...

"The thing I found most compelling about Mandan villages was that before the trappers and everybody came, there were some 10,000 Mandans up there and by the time Lewis and Clark got there, there were 1,000. And this happened all over the west, from smallpox and other diseases brought by the white men. It was a devastating thing to the Indians that, besides the white man coming in and taking their land, they were killing off their way of life and their population.

Another court martial took place on October 13th where John Newman was sentenced to 75 lashes and was banished from the party. His crime? He had *"uttered repeated expressions of a highly criminal and mutinous nature."* The Arikara chief was horrified by the whipping, since his people *"never whiped even their Children, from their burth."* Newman would be allowed to stay with the crew, along with Moses Reed who had been expelled earlier for desertion. Both men would be sent back to St. Louis in the spring; to do otherwise would have meant certain death.

On October 14th, the group spent their first night in present-day North Dakota. Progress remained slow as they fought the rain, wind, and cold. Fortunately, elk and bison herds were plentiful, but several of the creeks that flow into the Missouri were brackish enough to act as a laxative on anyone drinking from them. A grizzly bear was encountered on October 20th, but efforts to kill it proved fruitless.

Snow began falling on October 21st, five days before they reached the first Mandan village at the mouth of the Knife River. White men were nothing new to the Mandans since French and British fur trappers had been trading with them for many years. However, as had been the case with many Indian encounters along the way, York intrigued the Mandans.

Lewis visited the second Mandan village soon afterwards. Besides these two villages, there were three Hidatsa villages near the Knife River. With a total population of about 4,500 in the area, this was where the Corps wanted to spend the winter. Without the help of the Indians, it is doubtful the Expedition could have survived the winter facing them.

A council was held with members of the Mandan, Hidatsa, and Arikara tribes on *"a fair fine morning after Brackfast."* As usual, members of the Corps wore their dress uniforms, firing their guns and performing drills to impress the Indians. They also demonstrated wonders such as magnets and Lewis' air gun. The captains gave their standard speech about how the land was now ruled by the United States government, and that the Great Father (Thomas Jefferson) wanted peace among all Indian nations. Furthermore, Jefferson wanted the Indians to quit trading with Great Britain. The chiefs then received numerous gifts such as uniform coats, cocked hats, medals, flags, etc. After the speeches, a Mandan boy set fire to the prairie which spread so fast that a man and woman were caught and burnt to death, while three others were severely burned.

With one exception, all the French boatmen that had been hired to help get the boats up the Missouri River were discharged on November 3rd (one was enlisted as a private to replace John

Newman who had been expelled three weeks earlier). Most of the Frenchmen headed downriver, but a few decided to stay and go back with the return party in spring.

On November 4th, Toussaint Charbonneau was hired as an interpreter with the understanding he would bring one of his two wives. While he had no particular skills, he had lived with the Hidatsas for five years and both of his wives were Shoshone (Snake) Indians. The captains now realized there was no water route to the Pacific; they would need to obtain horses from the Shoshone Indians to cross the Rocky Mountains in 1805, so having someone who could translate would be invaluable.

The Corps decided to build winter quarters downstream from the first Mandan village since other potential sites lacked an adequate supply of wood. A triangular log stockade, with cabins along two walls, was built and named Fort Mandan. Winter arrived in full force by mid-November when ice began to form on the Missouri, just two weeks after the Corps decided to stop. Temperatures as low as 45 degrees below zero slowed construction, and the fort wasn't completed until Christmas.

Next episode we will learn more about the Mandan-Hidatsa villages. They were a major trade center and, during the winter months, Lewis and Clark would learn a lot about what to expect west of there as they talked to visitors.

INTERIOR OF THE HUT OF A MANDAN CHIEF, BY KARL BODMER

The interior of the lodge was spacious, tolerably light and clean. The outer wall of the lodge was formed by a ring of a dozen or more posts, four or five feet in height, with beams resting in the notch at the top of each post. At the center of the lodge was a small circular fire pit.

... how cold is it? ...

"They talk about how cold it was there and I think the coldest you get is 45 degrees below zero. You think, 'How would they get that?' Well, they had five thermometers, five glass thermometers that they left with, and I don't know when they broke the last one, but they stopped recording temperatures somewhere out in Montana, because they broke the thermometers. They'd only go down to 45 below and that's as cold as they could measure. And I still don't know if I've ever seen a thermometer you buy in a store that goes that low."

EPISODE 8

A Tough, Long Winter at Fort Mandan

On October 31, 1804, Captain Lewis wrote, "*The river being very low and the season so far advanced that it frequently shuts up with ice in this climate we determined to spend the Winter in this neighbourhood.*"

After six months of travel up the Missouri River, the Corps of Discovery found themselves in the ideal location to make camp. If their progress had been better, they might have kept going past the five Mandan and Hidatsu Indian villages near the mouth of the Knife River, 60 miles north of present-day Bismarck, North Dakota. Doing so might well have been disastrous.

Since other potential sites lacked an adequate supply of wood, the Corps decided to build their winter quarters downstream from the first Mandan village. Winter arrived in full force, just two weeks after the Corps decided to stop. Ice began to form on the Missouri River, and temperatures as low as 45 degrees below zero soon became a serious problem.

About 1,000 Mandan Indians were living in two villages in 1804, but an estimated 10,000 Mandans had lived in nine villages just 50 years earlier. Smallpox, introduced by white traders, had decimated their numbers, and the powerful Teton Sioux had forced them to abandon their settlements and move upriver where they merged with the Hidatsu (Minnetaree) tribe for security.

Early Day Farmers Market

Other Indian tribes living on the Great Plains were nomadic and lived off the land. The Mandans lived in permanent houses and grew more corn, beans, and squash than they needed. The Mandan and Hidatsu villages had become a major trading center that was visited by fur traders from Canada and St. Louis, along with several tribes from across the northern plains. Because of this, Lewis and Clark would learn a lot about what lay ahead on their journey to the Pacific Ocean as they gathered information while waiting for winter to pass.

How Cold is it?

Nobody was prepared for the winter ahead. Most of the men were from Virginia where snow is not unusual, but they had never seen weather like they were going to experience the next three months. By mid-November, they had abandoned their thin canvas tents and moved into the wood structures under

National Park Service photo

A reconstructed 40-foot diameter Mandan earthen lodge. The lodge was created by laying a matting, fabricated from willow sticks and bark, over a framework of posts and beams. A layer of dried prairie grass was spread over the matting, with an outer covering of thick sod.

construction. On December 8th, Clark wrote, "*a verry Cold morning, the Thermometer Stood at 12 d. below 0 which is 44 d. below the freesing point.*" Four days later it was 38 degrees below zero, but by December 14th it had warmed up to where "*the Murckerey Stood at 0.*" Then, at sunrise on December 17th, it was 45 degrees below zero and at "*about 8 oClock PM the thermometer fell to 74 d. below the freesing pointe.*"

Fort Mandan consisted of eight cabins inside an 18-foot tall stockade. The cabins were 14 feet square and each had a stone fireplace. The cracks in the walls were filled with mud to keep drafts out. A loft in each cabin was raised 7 feet off the floor and covered with grass and clay to provide warm sleeping quarters. Temperatures were below zero on 16 mornings in December, with just one day where temperatures were above freezing when the men awoke! It was so cold the men could only work an hour at a time and Fort Mandan was not completed until Christmas Day.

Turn up the Heat

The Indians had learned how to cope with the extremely cold temperatures by building dome-shaped earth lodges with a vent at the top. A fire in the center kept the room quite warm. Their lodges were large enough for several families (10 to 15 people), and during extremely cold periods the Indians brought their horses inside.

Besides shelter, food was a critical need. Meat was reasonably plentiful, and the Indians had dried fruits and vegetables. But was there enough corn to supply their own needs plus the needs of the Expedition members? Big White, the chief of the lower Mandan village, had told Lewis and Clark, "*if we eat you shall eat, if we Starve you must Starve also.*" Here again, we see proof Indians played a major role in the success of the Expedition.

While the fort was being built, half the men went hunting. Several hunters injured their hips by slipping in the snow while packing the meat back to the fort. Others suffered serious frostbite. Despite snow a foot deep, they succeeded in killing more than 30 buffalo, enough to last until February.

It must have been a lonely Christmas at Fort Mandan, so far from home and family. Each member of the party fired off three volleys of gunshots on Christmas morning. Clark issued two glasses of brandy to each man and allowed the cannon to be fired when the flag was raised. A third glass was issued later that morning, followed by a Christmas dinner that was "*the Best to eat that could be had,*" according to John Ordway.

..."welcome the New year"...

While hibernating and celebrating, Lewis and Clark were also anticipating the challenges that lay ahead. Trappers, traders, and Indians all convinced them they'd need horses, not canoes and a keelboat, to continue their journey. Hence, the value of the otherwise-dispensable Charbonneau and his two Snake Indian wives.

Joseph Whitehorse wrote "*The men then prepared one of the Rooms, and commenced dancing, we having with us Two Violins & plenty of Musicans in our party.*" Clark said the celebration "*Continued until 9 oClock P,M, when the frolick ended &c.*"

A Toast to the New Year

A week later, Patrick Gass wrote, "*Two shot were fired from this swivel* [cannon], *followed by a round of small arms, to welcome the New year. Captain Lewis then gave each a glass of good old whiskey, and a short time after another was given by Captain Clarke.*"

The men were allowed to go to one of the Mandan villages to dance. Clark wrote, "*I ordered my black Servent to Dance which amused the Croud verry much, and Some what astonished them, that So large a man Should be active &c. &.*" John Ordway wrote that "*a frenchman danced on his head.*" A third round of whiskey was issued later that day.

While the men wore several layers of clothing and stuffed fur into their clothing and buckskin moccasins, some still suffered from mild frostbite. Several men suffered more severe frostbite and were treated by Captain Lewis. Several Indians also received treatment. Typically, Lewis placed the frostbitten foot or hand into a bowl of cold water (this was the wrong thing to do, but was standard practice of the day).

Nobody from the Expedition lost so much as a toe, but some Indians were not so fortunate. On January 10th Clark wrote, "*last night was excessively Cold – the murkery this morning Stood at 40 d. below 0 which is 72 d. below the freesing point... Indians of the lower Villages turned out to hunt for a man & a boy who had not returned from the hunt yesterday, and borrowed a Slay to bring them in expecting to find them frosed to death...*" the 13 year old boy was found and brought "*to the fort with his feet frozed, having Stayed out all night without fire, with no other Covering than a Small Robe, goat skin leagens & a pr. Buffalow Skin mockersons.*" Lewis attempted to save his toes, but on January 27th he "*took of the Toes of one foot*" and four days later he "*Sawed off the boys toes*" on his other foot. Patrick Gass wrote of men who "*had their faces so badly frost bitten that that the skin came off.*"

It would be a long, tough winter. In the next episode, we'll learn about Sacajawea.

Pointing the way westward

The most famous statue of Sacajawea was sculpted by Alice Cooper (Hubbard), of Denver, Colorado, and was dedicated during the 1905 Lewis and Clark Centennial in Portland, Oregon. The heroic-sized statue contains 20 tons of copper. It was moved to Portland's Washington Park in 1906.

EPISODE 9

The Indispensable Sacajawea

There are more statues of Sacajawea in the United States than of any other woman. She has appeared in paintings and films, on postage stamps and on a golden dollar coin introduced in 2000. Nobody knows what she really looked like, but we have all heard the embellished stories of the teenager who carried her baby across half the continent and back while guiding the Lewis and Clark Expedition. In truth, while she did little, if any, guiding, her presence undoubtedly contributed to the success of the Expedition. Without her, the Lewis & Clark Expedition would have likely ended in failure.

Sacajawea, Sakakawea, or Sacagawea?

What is the correct spelling for the name of the American Indian woman who accompanied Lewis and Clark on their western journey 200 years ago? That depends on which source one consults; there is no uniform consensus. "Sacajawea" is the Shoshone spelling and means "boat pusher" while "Sakakawea" is the Hidatsa spelling and means "bird woman." Lewis and Clark had no idea how to spell it; they usually referred to her as "Squar" or "Indian Woman."

The few times they attempted to write her name, they spelled it phonetically. In 1805, Lewis wrote that they named a river after her in present-day Montana, *"this stream we called Sah-ca-gar-we-ah or bird woman's River, after our interpreter the Snake woman."* Thus, many people believe the Hidatsa pronunciation ("Tsakaka-wea") is correct. However, in 1825 Captain Clark made a list of the expedition members where he wrote, *"Se car ja we au – Dead."* Today, most people spell it Sacagawea, but we will use Sacajawea in this book to conform with the spelling of the lake in the center of Longview, Washington.

Subject to Interpretation

One of the first things Lewis and Clark did in November 1804 when they arrived at the Mandan Indian villages in present-day North Dakota was to hire a French-Canadian fur trader named Toussaint Charbonneau as an interpreter through his wife. Charbonneau, born about 1758, could not speak English, but he did speak a little Hidatsa. There were other Frenchmen they could have hired, but Charbonneau had something that Lewis and Clark knew would be most valuable in the coming year — he had two Shoshone wives.

... oral traditions ...

"The Indians told Lewis and Clark they'd have to get horses if they were to go all the way to the ocean. Lewis and Clark said, 'How are we going to get them from these Indians? We can't speak their language.' Charbonneau's two wives had both been kidnapped by Hidatsa Indians who sold them to the French trapper. He had no skills whatsoever, but in order to join the Expedition as an interpreter, the captains insisted he bring one of his wives. The part I find most ironic is here's one that's six months pregnant and they don't say, 'No, we don't want the baby on a journey.' You'd think they would've said, 'Bring the other one.'"

A Big Disappointment

During the first weeks at the Mandan villages, they had talked with many Indians and had come to realize there was no direct water route to the Pacific Ocean. It was clear they would have to portage across the Stoney (Rocky) Mountains. The Shoshone (Snake) Indians lived near the headwaters of the Missouri and had horses that Lewis and Clark would need to make the passage. But, to obtain horses, they would need some way to communicate with the Shoshones.

Charbonneau was hired on the condition he bring one of his wives with him. The fact the two captains didn't care which wife he brought seems a little surprising because one of his wives (Sacajawea) was six months pregnant and would give birth to a son just two months before the Expedition resumed their trek to the Pacific in April 1805. They just wanted someone who could speak Shoshone. Even then, communication would be difficult — Captains Lewis or Clark would speak to Private Francois Labiche, who would repeat it in French to Charbonneau who would then translate it to Hidatsa so Sacajawea could translate it into Shoshone. By the time the answer came back, six translations would take place, so errors were bound to creep in.

Oral Traditions

Surprisingly little is known about Sacajawea. Indians did not keep written histories, so the journals kept by the men of the Lewis and Clark Expedition and a few letters and records kept after the journey was over are the only factual information modern-day researchers can rely on. But, there are several oral histories about Sacajawea that have been passed down among different Indian tribes over the last 200 years that offer tantalizing (and often conflicting) information that makes it impossible to know for sure what the truth is.

While no records exist, it is likely Sacajawea was born in 1788 near present-day Salmon, Idaho. Shoshone Indians made annual trips into present-day Montana to dig roots and hunt for buffalo, elk, and deer. In 1800, while at their summer camp west of present-day Bozeman, Montana, Sacajawea and several other Shoshone girls were taken captive by a band of marauding Indians and later sold to some Hidatsa Indians who lived near the Mandan villages in North Dakota.

One of the kidnapped girls escaped enroute, but Sacajawea believed it would be impossible to find the way back to her people and accepted her fate as a 12-year-old captive. She learned the Hidatsa language and was adopted into their tribe. When just 14, she was sold (or lost in a gambling bet) to Charbonneau. A year later, she was pregnant and told to prepare for the long trip.

... reunited with her birth tribe ...

Translation among the captains and the Indians resembled the modern party game of "Telephone." Sacajawea could speak Hidatsa and Snake which she addressed to her husband Charbonneau. Charbonneau's languages were Hidatsa and French, so the co-captains used the French engages, who spoke English and French, to address Charbonneau.

The Sacagawea dollar (also known as the "golden dollar") is a United States dollar coin that has been minted every year since 2000, although not released for general circulation from 2002 through 2008 and again from 2012 onward due to its general unpopularity with the public and low business demand for the coin. These coins have a copper core clad by manganese brass, giving them a distinctive golden color.

On February 11, 1805, Sacajawea gave birth to a boy. It was a long and difficult labor, so Captain Lewis was called to help. A French trader told him a small portion of the rattle from a rattlesnake would hasten the birth process. Since her pain was so violent, Lewis reluctantly administered two rings of the rattle and within 10 minutes the baby was delivered. Charbonneau named him Jean Baptiste after his father, but his Indian name was Pomp, meaning "first born."

After leaving Fort Mandan in April 1805, it took four months for the Corps of Discovery to reach the place Sacajawea had been captured five years earlier. She began to recognize familiar landmarks and told Lewis and Clark they were getting close to the Shoshone lands. In August, Sacajawea was reunited with her birth tribe. One of the women who rushed to greet her was the girl who had escaped after Sacajawea was captured. The journals state the chief of the Shoshone tribe turned out to be Sacajawea's brother, but since all men in the tribe were referred to as brothers, fathers, or grandfathers, there is some question if he was her biological brother.

A tense moment occurred shortly after Sacajawea returned to her people. Lewis wrote, "*The father frequently disposes of his infant daughters in marriage to men who are grown or to men who have sons for whom they think proper to provide wives. the compensation given in such cases usually consists of horses or mules which the father receives at the time of contract and converts to his own uce. the girl remains with her parents untill she is conceived to have obtained the age of puberty which with them is considered to be the age of 13 or 14 years... Sah-car-gar-we-ah had been thus disposed of before she was taken by the Minnetares, or had arrived to the years of puberty. the husband was yet living and with this band. he was more than double her age and had two other wives. He claimed her as his wife but said that as she had had a child by another man, who was Charbono, that he did not want her.*"

Surprisingly, Sacajawea showed little or no interest in staying with her people. Most of her family was dead, and she had enjoyed life with the Hidatsa Indians. When the Expedition returned from the Pacific in 1806, they found no trace of the Shoshone Indians. Thus, Sacajawea returned to the Mandan villages with Charbonneau and their son and probably never saw her native family again.

... all iced up ...

"They made a mistake and left the boats in the water and they froze in place and the part that's also kind of funny is you've got a boat that's in the water here when the ice comes along, but then the water quits flowing. The water drops down, another layer of ice forms with air between. So they had to chip through multiple layers to get their boats out."

EPISODE 10

Baby, It's Cold Outside

Many of us have heard weather reports of the extraordinarily low temperatures experienced in the upper Midwest. When the Lewis & Clark Expedition was camped at Fort Mandan (near present-day Bismark, North Dakota), they recorded temperatures as low as minus 45 degrees on several nights in 1805 (that was as low as their thermometer went!). Does it still get that cold? On January 30, 2019, it got down to minus 27 at today's reconstructed Fort Mandan – and that same morning, it got down to minus 56 degrees in Cotton, Minnesota. Those are actual temperatures, not the hyped "wind-chill" factors we often hear about. Nowadays, people live in insulated homes heated by natural gas, oil or electricity... but, that is still cold!

All Iced Up

After spending five months in present-day North Dakota during a bitterly cold winter, the Corps of Discovery was anxious to continue their journey to the Pacific Ocean. They had made a major mistake by leaving their keelboat and two smaller pirogues in the Missouri River after arriving at the site of Fort Mandan in November, 1804. With temperatures down to 45 degrees below zero, it hadn't taken long for the boats to become trapped in the ice.

On January 22, 1805, the men began trying to chop the boats out, but they soon realized it was not going to be easy. The fluctuating level of the river had resulted in several layers of ice, and as soon as they chopped through one layer the void filled with water. An attempt was made to heat large rocks in the fire and then place them in the boats to melt the ice; however, upon placing the cold rocks in the fire, they exploded. It took over a month of chopping to free the boats, just as the ice was breaking up. If they hadn't managed to get them out at that time, the boats would almost certainly have been crushed as the ice began breaking up and moving downriver.

March 5th was the first day the temperature reached 40 degrees in 1805. The boats were put back in the water on April 1st, 1805, and the next week was spent packing. The Missouri was too shallow to take the keelboat any further, so it was loaded with all the mineral and botanical specimens, animal skeletons and skins (along with some live animals) collected between St. Louis and Fort Mandan. Many of those items are still on display at Jefferson's home at Monticello and in the Smithsonian. Jefferson planted some of the seeds, and many of those plants are still growing at Monticello. Clark had spent all winter drawing a map of the area west of the Mississippi River, based on his

The obverse design for the 2005 nickel commemorating the Lewis and Clark bicentennial contained a new likeness of America's third president, Thomas Jefferson. The "Liberty" inscription on the coin is based upon Jefferson's own handwriting. The reverse featured the American bison. Expedition journals described the buffalo as an animal of great significance to many American Indian cultures. Nickels minted between 1913 and 1938 also had a buffalo on the reverse, while an Indian was depicted on the front; many people feel it was one of America's most beautiful coins.

The Indian depicted on the so-called "buffalo nickel" is a composite of three Indian chiefs: Two Moons, John Big Tree, and Iron Tail, the chief that faced Custer at the Little Big Horn. Creators of the coin wished to capture a Native American portrait but not to associate the facial features with any specific tribe.

observations and information obtained from Indians and fur traders. A copy of that map was sent to Jefferson, along with a 45,000 word report, when the keelboat headed back to St. Louis with 15 men of the return party on April 7, 1805.

On the road again

On that same day, the 33 members of the permanent party, including Sacajawea and her 55-day old son, began the journey up the Missouri into uncharted territory. Lewis wrote, "*Our vessels consisted of six small canoes, and two large pirogues. This little fleet altho' not quite so rispectable as those of Columbus or Capt. Cook, were still viewed by us with as much pleasure as those deservedly famed adventurers ever beheld theirs... we were now about to penetrate a country at least two thousand miles in width, on which the foot of civilized man had never trodden.*"

On April 9th, Clark wrote, "*I saw a Musquetor to day*" and the following day he wrote "*Misquetors troublesom.*" This is surprising since it had been so cold all winter; all precipitation between October 15 and March 23 had been snow. After fighting mosquitoes the previous year, this was a bad omen! On April 14th, they reached "*the highest point to which any whiteman had ever ascended.*" From that point on, only Sacajawea had first-hand knowledge of what lay ahead.

Grizzly Claw

... covered with herds ...

The Corps of Discovery hunted for their livelihood. In his book titled 'The Natural History of the Lewis and Clark Expedition,' Raymond Darwin Burroughs tallied the game consumed during the course of the Expedition: Deer 1,001; Elk 375; Bison 227; Antelope 62; Big Horn Sheep 35; Grizzly Bears 43; Black Bears 23; Beaver (shot or trapped) 113; Otter 16; Geese and Brant 104; Grouse 46; Turkeys 9; Plovers 48; Wolves (only one eaten) 18; Indian Dogs (purchased and consumed) 190; Horses, 12.

EPISODE 11

Just the Grizzly Facts, Ma'am

In the spring of 1805, the Lewis and Clark Expedition was preparing to resume their trek to the Pacific Ocean after spending the winter near the Mandan and Hidatsu Indian villages. Fort Mandan was located 45 miles upstream from present-day Bismark, North Dakota.

After the Corps of Discovery left St. Louis a year earlier, in May 1804, their progress up the Missouri River had been very slow. Due to the heavily laden boats and fast current, they averaged only seven miles per day until reaching the Mandan Villages where they spent the winter. When they continued their westward journey on April 7, 1805, they did so with fewer men and supplies, and without the heavy keelboat. They had two pirogues from the previous year plus six dugout canoes they carved from cottonwood logs.

The smaller boats and lighter load made it possible to cover upwards of 25 miles per day. Headwinds were a problem, but strong tailwinds allowed the crews to raise the sails and cover great distances on several days. On April 24th, Clark wrote, "*The wind blew so hard during the whole of this day, that we were unable to move.*" Clark later wrote "*The party complain much of the Sand in their eyes, the Sand is verry fine and rises in clouds from the Points and bars of the river, I may Say during those winds we eat Drink & breeth a prepotion of Sand.*" Fine alkali dust and constant glare of the sun on the water probably caused the sore eyes.

The land was mostly open grasslands, with a few trees growing along the river. The further west they went, the more wildlife they saw. On April 25th, Lewis wrote, "*the whol face of the country was covered with herds of Buffaloe, Elk & Antelopes; deer are also abundant... the buffaloe Elk and Antelope are so gentle that we pass near them while feeding, without appearing to excite any alarm among them, and when we attract their attention, they frequently approach us more nearly to discover what we are.*"

On April 26th, they reached the mouth of the Yellowstone River, five miles from present-day Montana. An extra ration of whiskey was served; the fiddles came out, and the men sang and danced in celebration. By mid-May, they had covered about 350 miles, reaching an area now covered by Fort Peck Lake, near Glasgow, Montana.

Grin and bear it

While Lewis and Clark spent the winter at Fort Mandan, Indians told them of a ferocious bear they would encounter. On April 17th Lewis wrote, "*tho' we continue to see many tracks of the bear we have seen but very few of them, and those are at a*

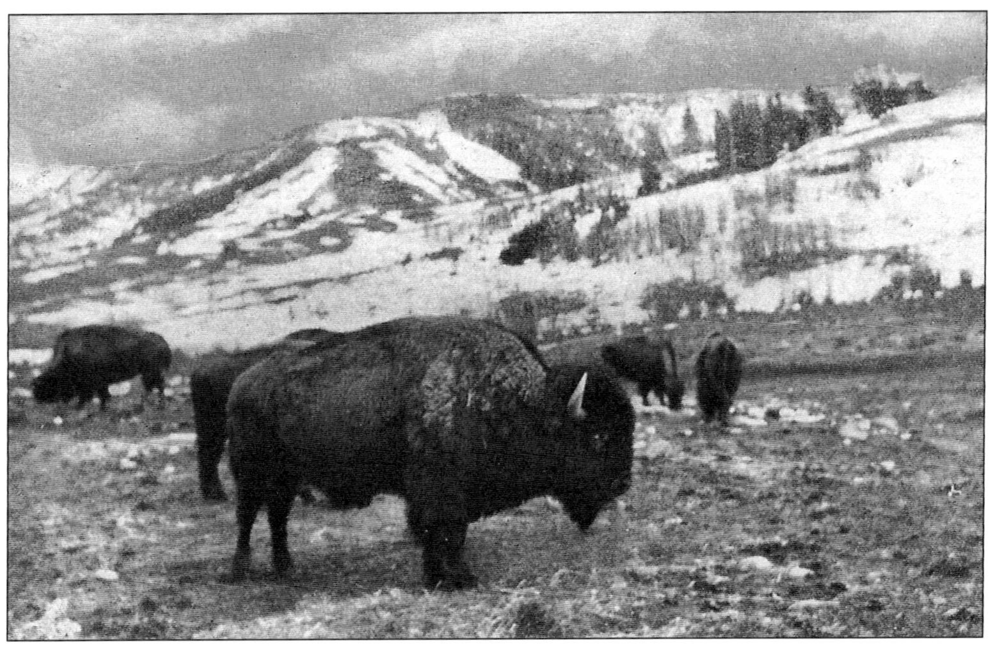

Snow near Fort Mandan was slow to melt. POSTCARD FROM THE AUTHOR'S PRIVATE COLLECTION.

great distance generally running from us; I thefore presume that they are extremely wary and shy; the Indian account of them dose not corrispond with our experience so far."

Two weeks later, after trying to kill two Grizzly bears, Lewis wrote, *"one of them made his escape, the other after my firing on him pursued me seventy or eighty yards, but fortunately had been so badly wounded that he was unable to pursue so closely as to prevent my charging my gun; we again repeated our fir and killed him. It was a male not fully grown, we estimated his weight at 300 lbs...It is astonishing to see the wounds they will bear before they can be put to death."*

Despite these encounters, Lewis still felt the bears were over-rated. On April 29th he wrote, *"the Indians may well fear this anamal equiped as they generally are with their bows and arrows or indifferent fuzees* [inferior muskets], *but in the hands of skillfull riflemen they are by no means as formidable or dangerous as they have been represented."* However, his assessment would soon be revised.

Later that week Clark wrote, *"In the evening we Saw a Brown or grisley beare on a Sand beech, I went out with one man Geo. Drewyer & Killed the bear, which was verry large and a terrible looking animal, which we found verry hard to kill. We Shot ten balls into him before we killed him, & 5 of those Balls through his lights* [lungs]. *We had nothing that could way him, I think his weight may be Stated at 500 pounds, he measured 8 feet 7-1/2 In. from his nose to the extremity of the Toe... 3 feet 11 Ins. arround the neck. His talents* [talon, or claw] *was 4 Inches & 3/8 long. Captain Lewis thought the Grizzly weighted 600 pounds."*

Another Grizzly proved hard to kill when Lewis reported a man *"had shot a brown bear which immediately turned on him and pursued him a considerable distance but he had wounded it so badly that it could not overtake him. I immediately turned out with seven of the party in quest of this monster, we at length found his trale and persued him about a mile by the blood through very thick brush... and shot him through the skull with two balls."*

After that adventure, Lewis changed his mind about the Grizzly when he wrote, *"I must confess that I do not like the gentlemen and had rather fight two Indians than one bear."* It was next to impossible to kill a Grizzly with one shot; a direct shot to the head or lungs was not enough. And, since it took a minute or more to reload their guns, a second shot was often not possible.

While Clark referred to it as a *"grisly beare,"* he was not responsible for the scientific name Ursus arctos horribilis. However, I'm sure he would have approved!

THE *Divide*

"Handsome Falls," renamed Rainbow Falls by a railroad surveyor in 1872, had a 47-foot drop. It was one of the five major waterfalls encountered by the Lewis and Clark Expedition at present-day Great Falls, Montana. Dams have diverted the water to generate electricity, but it is possible to see where some of the falls used to be. The railroad bridge shown in this picture was built in 1901, and the dam was completed in 1910.

EPISODE 12

On the Road Again after a Winter at Fort Mandan

On April 7 of 1805, the Corps of Discovery resumed their westward trek after wintering at Fort Mandan. During the winter of 1804, Lewis and Clark had pulled together all available information about what might lie ahead. Besides the maps they brought from St. Louis and obtained from several explorers, they recorded information from Indians. They had great hopes the maps they would be relying on were accurate. As they made their way across present-day North Dakota and Montana, they were pleased to find rivers where the Indians had told them they would be. Progress up the Missouri River after leaving Fort Mandan was better than expected. The Corps reached the present-day border between North Dakota and Montana on April 26th.

Don't Rock the Boat!

On May 14, 1805, disaster struck the white pirogue. In it were Sacajawea and Pomp, along with her husband Charbonneau, and five other men. Clark wrote, *"a Squawl of wind Struck our Sale broad Side and turned the perogue nearly over, and... She nearly filed with water – the articles which floated out was nearly all caught by the Squar who was in the rear. This accident had like to have cost us deerly; for in this perogue were embarked, our papers, Instruments, books, medicine, a great proportion of our merchandize, and in short almost every article indispensably necessary to... insure the success of the enterprise."*

Lewis tells us, *"Charbono was at the helm of this Perogue... Charbono cannot swim and is perhaps the most timid waterman in the world... Capt. C. and myself were both on shore... spectators of her fate."* Charbonneau panicked as the wind *"turned her... topsaturva. Capt. C. and myself both fired our guns to attract the attention..., but they did not hear us... they suffered the perogue to lye on her side for half a minute before they took the sail in, the perogue then wrighted but had filled within an inch of the gunwales; Charbono still crying to his god for mercy, had not yet recollected the rudder, nor could the repeated orders of the Bowsman, Cruzat, bring him to his recollection until he threatened to shoot him instantly if he did not take hold of the rudder and do his duty."* Two men bailed out the water with kettles as the other three rowed to shore. A very close call, but it wasn't the first time; just a month earlier, Charbonneau had almost overturned the same boat under similar conditions.

Contemporary photo of the confluence of Marias and Missouri Rivers.

... what to do? ...

Lewis and Clark's trailblazing and orientation continue to amaze students of the Expedition and so does their most notable conundrum: what to do and where to go at the confluence of what is now the Marias and Missouri Rivers. Today, the spot is memorialized as Decision Point, a significant stop on the Lewis and Clark National Historic Trail.

Capt. Clark: Romance on his mind?

On May 29th, while traveling through the Missouri River Breaks section now designated a National Wild and Scenic River, Clark named the "Judith River" in honor of Julia (Judy) Hancock, a 13-year old girl in Virginia he would marry three years later. Captain Lewis mentioned it in his journal and while he probably didn't approve of naming the river after a young girl, two weeks later he did a similar thing.

Is this the way to the Great Falls?

On June 2nd, near present-day Loma, Montana, they came upon a fork in the river not shown on their maps. The Captains had been told there was only one major northern river between the Mandan villages and the Great Falls of the Missouri; the Indians called it *"the river which scolds at all others."* The Corps had passed such a river three weeks earlier and named it the Milk River due to its white color. So, what was this "extra" river doing here?

Lewis wondered which river the Indians *"had discribed to us as approaching very near to the Columbia river. To mistake the stream... and to ascend such stream to the rocky Mountain or perhaps much further before we could inform ourselves whether it did approach the Columbia or not, and then be obliged to return and take the other stream would not only loose us the whole of this season but would probably so dishearten the party that it might defeat the expedition altogether."*

If the Missouri went north, then why hadn't the Indians told them of the river coming in from the south? Both rivers were about the same size since it was peak runoff. The north fork was muddy while the south fork was clear. The north fork was deeper, but was a little narrower and slower-flowing. The Indians had told them *"that the water of the Missouri was nearly transparent at the great falls"* so Lewis and Clark were sure the south fork was the true Missouri. However, everyone else felt the Missouri was actually the north fork. What to do?

Management/Labor Negotiations

A small party was sent up each fork in an effort to determine which was the major stream, but they returned the same day with no conclusive information. Lewis and Clark could have simply ordered the men to proceed up the south fork, but they decided to each take a small party to *"ascend these rivers until we could perfectly satisfy ourselves of the one, which it would be most expedient for us to take on our main journey to the Pacific."*

Crooked Falls is one of five falls on the Missouri River known collectively as Great Falls, which drop a total of 612 feet in ten miles. Meriwether Lewis said they were the grandest sight he had beheld thus far on their journey. POSTCARD FROM THE AUTHOR'S PRIVATE COLLECTION.

... the agreeable sound of a fall of water ...

"They could hear it. So it must have been amazing to see Great Falls before it was dammed up and for the Expedition to cross the prairie and see this big cloud of water vapor and hear the roar. It makes you appreciate how things were before we came along and changed it. They heard the roar long before they saw this and the same is true when they came to the mouth of the Columbia. They heard the roar of the ocean at Skamokawa."

By June 8th, after both parties had returned, there still was no definitive answer. Lewis wrote that the men, *"said very cheerfully that they were ready to follow us anywhere we thought proper to direct, but that they still thought that the other was the river and that they were afraid the South fork would soon terminate in the mountains and leave us a great distance from the Columbia."* As it would turn out, both groups would be right – the south fork was the true Missouri, but taking it would still leave the Corps with a very difficult overland passage across the Rocky Mountains. After spending a week deliberating about which route to take, the Captains decided to proceed up the south fork.

Party Time!

Lewis wrote, *"wishing that if we were in error to be able to detect it and rectify it as soon as possible it was agreed..."* that Lewis *"should set out with a small party by land up the South fork and continue our rout up it until we found the falls or reached the snowy mountains."* Lewis named the north fork "Maria's River" in honor of a cousin. Later they found out the reason the Indians had failed to tell the Corps about the Marias river was because they always cut across the plains on horses and never saw where it joins the Missouri.

A dram of whiskey was passed out and the men danced around the campfire as Pierre Cruzatte played his fiddle. The supply of whiskey was running low so only half a gill (2 ounces) was dispersed.

Do You Hear What I Hear?

Three days later, Lewis wrote, *"I had proceded on... whin my ears were saluted with the agreeable sound of a fall of water and advancing a little further I saw the spray arise above the plain like a column of smoke... which soon began to make a roaring too tremendous to be mistaken for any cause short of the great falls of the Missouri... I hurried down... to gaze on this sublimely grand specticle."*

Lewis sent a man back to tell Clark they were on the right river. And, he decided to explore upstream to find out where the best route around the falls might be. To his dismay, he found there were actually five major waterfalls, and many sets of rapids — dropping more than 600 feet in 10 miles — that would require an 18-mile overland portage. More on that next episode.

Lewis saw "a herd of at least a thousand buffaloe" and proceeded to shoot one.

POSTCARD FROM THE AUTHOR'S PRIVATE COLLECTION.

EPISODE 13

The Painful Portage

As we re-trace the steps of Lewis and Clark's Expedition, we join them near the Great Falls in present-day Montana, as they continued their journey towards the Pacific Ocean.

Delays and more delays

After reaching the mouth of the present-day Maria's River on June 2, 1805, the Corps spent over a week deciding which fork was the Missouri River. They proceeded up the south fork on June 11th and soon reached the Great Falls that the Indians had described. However, rather than just one waterfall, there were five. The Captains had only planned on spending one day to portage around the falls, but a full month would pass before they resumed their journey up the river.

Sacajawea had become very sick. Attempts to revive her included several bleedings with applications of quinine and opium. Her husband, Charbonneau, wanted to take her back to the Mandan villages, but Clark refused. Finally, after drinking mineral water from a nearby sulfur spring, Sacajawea recovered and was able to eat, but relapsed after eating too many apples and dried fish. Lewis *"rebuked Sharbono severely"* for letting her eat such food after being told what she was allowed to eat. Several doses of saltpeter and laudanum led to her recovery. Lewis and Clark were concerned about Sacajawea for two reasons. First, if she died, who would take care of her baby, Pomp? Secondly, and perhaps of greater concern, who would translate when they reached the Shoshone Indians near the headwaters of the Missouri River? The fate of the Corps of Discovery would rest on their ability to obtain horses from the Indians, and without Sacajawea there was little hope of making such a trade.

Big mistake

Grizzly bears presented a serious problem around the Great Falls. While exploring a possible portage route, Lewis saw *"a herd of at least a thousand buffaloe"* and proceeded to shoot one. While waiting for it to die, a large bear crept up behind Lewis to within 20 steps before he saw it. Lewis immediately raised his gun to shoot, but quickly remembered he had not reloaded. Lewis thought he might be able to reach a tree about 300 yards away, but when he turned the bear *"pitched at me, open mouthed and full speed, I ran about 80 yards... the idea struk me to get into the water to such debth that I could... defend myself with my espontoon... the moment I put myself in this attitude of defence he sudonly wheeled about as if frightened... and retreated,"* running three miles across the prairie. Lewis added, *"I felt myself not a little gratifyed that*

... the actual portage ...

"The portage was a huge effort that might have been avoided. The Indians didn't go by boat. The Indians went by horse — that's the thing that Lewis and Clark found out later. They had spent two weeks getting to the Great Falls, eighteen days portaging around, and then a month reaching the Snake Indians to see about the horses. When they get there, they're told, 'Well, if you just would've gone across the overland route it's only four days,' and they had spent close to two months getting from one point to the other."

Portage at the Great Falls – drawing on an interpretive sign at Sulphur Springs, Montana.

he had declined the combat. My gun reloaded I felt confidence once more... and determined never again to suffer my piece to be longer empty than the time she necessarily required to charge her."

Rough road ahead

Two carts were built to carry the dugout canoes. A large Cottonwood tree was cut into slices to make wheels, and the hardwood mast from the white pirogue was cut up to make axles. The actual portage began on June 21 and was completed on July 2. Thankfully, temperatures were mild (mid-seventies), so the men were not faced with heat exhaustion in addition to physical exhaustion. The canoes weighed at least 1,000 pounds, and after pulling them out of the Missouri River canyon, they were filled with cargo and pulled across the reasonably level 18-mile portage route. However, the ground was far from smooth. After heavy rains, buffalo left deep hoof prints in the mud, and the sharp edges of those dried out tracks cut into the feet of the men as they pulled the heavy carts. In addition, long spines of the Prickly Pear cactus poked through the bottoms and sides of the men's moccasins. Even after sewing a double thickness sole, their feet still looked like pin cushions. If that wasn't enough, rattlesnakes were a constant threat and at least one man was bitten.

A total of four round trips were required to portage everything around the Great Falls. The men were utterly exhausted. Lewis wrote, *"they are obliged to halt and rest frequently for a few minutes, at every halt these poor fellows tumble down and are so much fortiegued that many of them are asleep in an instant; in short their fatiegues are incredible; some are limping from the soreness of their feet, others faint and unable to stand for a few minutes, with heat and fatiegue, yet no one complains, all go with cheerfulness."* On the last two portage trips, the wind was strong and in the right direction to allow the men to raise the sail on two boats – literally, prairie schooners.

Hail to the Chief

On June 27th, the men were caught on the open prairie in a violent thunderstorm lasting two hours. Clark wrote that hail stones *"the size of a pigion's egg and not unlike them in form covered the ground to a debth of 1-1/2 inches — for about 20 minutes during this storm hail fell of an innomus size driven with violence almost incredible, when they struck the ground they would bound to the hight of ten to 12 feet and pass 20 or thirty before they touched again."* Clark reported some hail stones weighed almost a quarter pound and measured 7 inches in circumference (more than 2 inches in diameter); they were round and perfectly solid. Clark wrote, *"I*

... this horrible effort ...

"This is one of the few routes still walkable — and it's remarkable. You go up a creek off the Missouri to a steep little draw going upwards to the prairie above the Missouri River. Retracing that route, I was able for the first time in all my reading, to say, 'Okay, I'm now with them.' And I was aware of this horrible effort to get the wheeled boats up there, the hailstorms they had, this amazingly steep draw they had to get up. And I don't know how you'd get an empty boat up, let alone with all the tons of stuff they had. It was just mind-boggling and Clark or Lewis, I forget which one, writes about how the men had to stop and rest every few minutes they were so tired. Sweat just poured off them. They stop and they instantly go to sleep. They just lay down and collapse. They were exhausted, but yet they didn't complain. They get up and they do the job because that was what they were there for."

... some nearly killed ...

"The prickly pear were everywhere and those things have got spikes on them this long and they're down low. The prickly pear doesn't grow tall like a cactus, it stays low. So, these guys were out there pushing these things across these spiky things with only moccasins on. Then they get caught in a hailstorm and pulverized. It was just terrible."

am convinced if one of those had struck a man on the neaked head it would have knocked him down, if not fractured his skull." Clark issued an extra ration of whiskey that night.

Two days later another storm caught the men. This time, Clark led Sacajawea, Pomp, and Charbonneau to a deep ravine to seek shelter from the hail. Clark wrote, *"a torrent of rain and hail fell more violent than ever I Saw before."* While hiding under a rock ledge, they were almost swept away when a 15-foot wall of water roared down the ravine and caught them by surprise. Clark's slave, York, was not in the gully and thought they had been washed over the cliff into the Missouri. Several men were caught in the open during the storm, others abandoned the loaded canoes and ran for camp. Clark wrote, *"the hail & wind being So large and violent in the plains, and them naked, they were much bruised, and Some nearly killed – one knocked down three times, and others without hats or any thing on their heads bloodey & Complained veery much; I refreshed them with a little grog."* After the storm, the prairie was a sea of mud, making it impossible to move the carts. The portage was completed July 2nd – eleven days after they began. However, the journey up the Missouri would not be resumed until July 14th.

Next episode we'll learn about the "Experiment" that would cause the 12-day delay.

Armory Superintendent Joseph Perkins (left) and Captain Meriwether Lewis inspecting the collapsible iron boat frame built at Harpers Ferry in 1803.

BOTH ILLUSTRATIONS BY KEITH ROCCO
FOR HARPERS FERRY NATIONAL HISTORIC PARK. NATIONAL PARK SERVICE.

Joseph Fields, Capt. Lewis, Patrick Gass and John Shields stretching leather skins over the iron boat frame.

EPISODE 14

After Great Falls, the Fourth of July and a Failed Experiment

After a grueling eleven days portaging around the Great Falls, finishing on July 2, 1805, the men were exhausted and needed a rest. Thus, the Corps began celebrating Independence Day a little early. Pierre Cruzatte played his fiddle, and the men danced as they drank the last of the whiskey. While the men probably fired their guns, Mother Nature also made a little noise that day. Since their arrival at the falls, the men had repeatedly heard a noise resembling the discharge of a six-pound cannon at a distance of three miles. Initially, it was thought to be thunder. But, Lewis himself *"heard this noise very distinctly, it was perfectly calm, clear and not a cloud to be seen."* He heard three such discharges in an hour. The men had reported hearing up to seven discharges in quick succession. Interestingly, while these noises are still heard to this day, nobody has yet come up with a verifiable explanation.

A grand experiment

One of the more memorable lines in the 1975 movie "Jaws" was Police Chief Martin Brody telling Quint, "You're gonna need a bigger boat." Lewis and Clark had the opposite problem. As the Corps of Discovery traveled up the Missouri River, they would have to abandon their large boats as the river grew shallower.

Dugout canoes replaced the larger boats, but they were unstable and would not carry much of a load. Captain Lewis had foreseen this problem in 1803 while making plans for the expedition and designed what came to be called "The Experiment." The federal arsenal at Harper's Ferry, Virginia, constructed a portable iron boat frame that Lewis believed could be covered with buffalo hides and used to carry provisions when the water became too shallow for the heavy wooden boats.

While no drawings exist, records indicate the assembled boat was 36 feet long and 4-1/2 feet wide. The frame was made of wrought iron ribs that could be assembled with screws. According to Lewis' description, there were two designs used for the individual sections: one curved, or in the shape necessary for the stem and stern, the other semi-cylindrical, or in the form of those sections which constitute the body of the canoe. There were a total of eight sections, each about 4-1/2 feet long, that could be fastened together to make the boat frame. Each section weighed 22 pounds, for a total of 176 pounds of iron. The total weight of the iron, hides, wood, and bark needed for the entire boat would be 500 pounds.

... underestimated the time ...

"All they needed was pitch to seal it up. It would've been the cat's meow because when they loaded that thing up, when they first put it in the water when it didn't leak, it carried some 8,000 pounds of goods. But an hour later it was sinking."

In an 1805 letter to President Jefferson from Fort Mandan, Lewis wrote, "*Our baggage is all embarked on board six small canoes and two pirogues: we shall set out at the same moment that we dispatch the*" keelboat back to St. Louis. "*One or perhaps, both of these pirogues we shall leave at the falls of the Missouri, from whence we intend continuing our voyage in the canoes and a perogue of skins, the frame of which was prepared at Harper's Ferry. This perogue is now in a situation which will enable us to prepare it in the course of a few hours.*"

The best-laid plans

As Lewis predicted, the red pirogue was buried in a cache near the mouth of Maria's river on June 9th, and the white pirogue placed in a cache at the base of the Great Falls two weeks later. However, Lewis drastically underestimated the amount of time required to assemble the portable boat.

The first of the four portages made around the Great Falls began on June 21 and contained the materials to assemble the iron boat. Lewis already saw a problem: "*I readily perceive difficulties in preparing the leather boat which are the want of convenient and proper timber; bark, skins, and above all that of pitch to pay*" [seal] "*her seams, a deficiency that I really know not how to surmount...*" The frame was quickly assembled while the skins from 28 elk and four buffalo were prepared to cover it.

The final portage around the Great Falls was completed on July 2nd. Rather than resuming their journey up the Missouri River, construction of the iron boat was still not complete and would delay the expedition. While Lewis tried to find a source of pitch, the men shaved the hair off the elk skins. Attempts to extract pitch from pine logs that had floated down from the mountains were unsuccessful. Without pitch or tar, Lewis wrote, "*I fear the whole operation of my boat will be useless.*"

The hides were sewn together and then attached to the iron framework. On July 3rd, Lewis wrote, "*I fear I have committed another blunder also in sewing the skins with a nedle which has sharp edges, these have cut the skin and as it drys I discover that the throng dose not fill the holes as I expected.*" Using a round needle might have prevented the gaping holes.

Two days later, Lewis wrote, "*This morning I had the boat removed to an open situation, scaffold her off the ground, turned her keel to the sun and kindled fires under her to dry her more expediciously. I set a couple of men to pounding of charcoal to form a composition with some beeswax which we have and buffaloe tallow now my only hope and resource for paying my boat; I sincerely hope it may answer yet I feel it will not. The boat in every other rispect completely answers my most sanguine expectation; she is not yet dry and eight men carry her with the greatest ease; she is strong and will carry at least 8,000 lbs.*"

... cost the Expedition 12 days ...

"If they hadn't spent all the time on the portage and 12 days building the iron boat and getting over to get the horses and then getting back to the Lo Lo Pass, they would've made it over to the ocean that first year without any trouble at all. As it was, they were lucky just to get through the Rockies — it was snowing on them up there when they went across the Pass."

By July 8th, *"The boat was sufficiently dry to receive a coat of the composition which I accordingly applied. This adds very much to her appearance whether it will be effectual or not."* When they *"launched the boat, she lay like a perfect cork on the water."* By evening they *"discovered that a greater part of the composition had separated from the skins and left the seams of the boat exposed to the water and she leaked in such a manner that she would not answer."* Lewis wrote that the failure of the Experiment *"mortified me not a little."*

Lewis *"found that the section formed of the buffaloe hides on which some hair had been left, answered much the best purpose; this leaked but little and the parts which were well covered with hair about 1/8th of an inch in length retained the composition perfectly and remained sound and dry."* He now realized that shaving all the hair off the elk hides resulted in nothing for the beeswax and tallow concoction to bond with, but it was too late to start over.

It took five more days to carve two additional dugout canoes from cottonwood trees growing about 16 miles upstream. The "Experiment" had cost the expedition 12 days that would have been better spent traveling. The hides were removed and the iron frame put in a cache above Great Falls. When the journey resumed on July 14th, they were far behind schedule and had given up all hope of making it to the Pacific Ocean and back to Fort Mandan by that winter.

When the Corps returned a year later, Lewis found *"the iron frame of the boat had not suffered materially."* There is no mention of what they did with the iron frame, but it is possible they didn't leave it there since the metal would have been valuable to the expedition for trading with Indians. No trace of the iron boat has ever been found.

Next episode, we will arrive at the Shoshone village where Sacajawea had been kidnapped in 1800.

Gate of the Mountains, along Missouri River, Montana

Early rendering of Gates of the Mountain, declared a national wilderness in 1964 and formally designated Gates of the Mountains Wild Area.

POSTCARD FROM THE AUTHOR'S PRIVATE COLLECTION.

...the journey resumed...

Once past the painful portage, the Expedition sought the headwaters of the Missouri. Passing through what today is called the Gates of the Mountains Wilderness, which still exists relatively unchanged, Captain Lewis wrote on July 19, 1805: *'this evening we entered much the most remarkable cliffs that we have yet seen. these cliffs rise from the waters edge on either side perpindicularly to the height of 1,200 feet...the river appears to have forced its way through this immense body of solid rock for the distance of 5-3/4 Miles...I called it the Gates of the Rocky Mountains.'*

EPISODE 15

A Critical Time for the Expedition: Must Get Horses! Sacajawea Helps

After wasting 12 days trying to get Captain Lewis's experimental iron boat to float after portaging around the Great Falls in present-day Montana, the journey resumed on July 14, 1805. A week later Lewis saw smoke that he hoped meant Indians were nearby. When Sacajawea began to recognize familiar landmarks, everyone was encouraged. On July 27th, the expedition reached the headwaters of the Missouri at Three Forks, west of present-day Bozeman, Montana. This was where Sacajawea had been taken captive five years earlier, but there was no sign of her people.

Finally, on August 11th, they saw a lone Indian on horseback, the first Indian seen since leaving Fort Mandan four months earlier. Lewis tried to approach, but the Indian turned and galloped away.

On August 12, 1805, after traveling 3,000 miles since leaving St. Louis 20 months earlier, the Corps of Discovery had reached the Continental Divide (the border between Idaho and Montana). There they found a spring believed to be the highest source of water flowing into the Missouri River. They crossed over a ridge and Lewis drank from a stream he assumed, incorrectly, to be the headwaters of the Columbia River.

Its not going to be easy!

Lewis then went ahead to look for the hoped for one-day portage route between the Missouri and Columbia River drainages. Upon reaching the 7373-foot summit of Lemhi Pass, east of present-day Salmon, Idaho, Lewis *"discovered immence ranges of high mountains still to the West of us with their tops partially covered with snow."* He could see there was no Northwest Passage or easy walk to the Columbia River.

Lewis realized the fate of the Expedition now rested on their finding the Shoshone Indians and obtaining horses to continue the journey over the mountains and to the Columbia River's watershed. The previous day, Lewis had seen the first Indian since leaving Fort Mandan four months earlier. Two days later, contact was made with two Shoshone Indians. Lewis gave them a few gifts and, using sign language, convinced them to take him to the rest of their tribe. They soon met 60 warriors on horseback; after seeing the gifts, they welcomed Lewis and his small party. Lewis only had three men with him, so the Shoshone could have easily killed them if they wanted. Chief Cameahwait held a celebration that night.

... "immence ranges of high mountains"...

" They follow the Missouri up to the 'Stony Mountains.' They have to walk across this little hill and there they would find the mouth of the river going down to the Columbia. They found a spring, drank water from it, and made a note saying 'I drank water from the headwaters of the Columbia,' but then they go a little further up the pass and look out and as far as they can see are mountains. Not just mountains, but snow-capped. The things are full of snow and they know it's going to be a very difficult traverse."

I'd prefer medium-rare

The next day, in order to give Captain Clark and the rest of the men time to catch up, Lewis and his men went hunting with some of the Indians. When word came back to camp that Drouillard had killed a deer, the Indians raced off on horses. Lewis wrote that by the time he arrived, *"Each Indian had a piece of some discription and all eating most ravenously. Some were eating kidnies, the melt* [spleen] *and liver, blood running from the corners of their mouths."* Meat was very scarce, and the Indians had been living off berries and fish, so they devoured the whole deer without bothering to cook it.

Trust but verify?

When Lewis told of more white men coming upriver, the Indians became suspicious. They feared an ambush by the Blackfeet Indians. To reduce their anxiety, Lewis and his men exchanged clothing with the Indians, and went so far as to give them their rifles with instructions to shoot them if it was a trap. Lewis told Cameahwait one of their people, Sacajawea, was with Clark. He also told about York, Clark's black slave. The Indians were eager to see such a man.

Family Reunion

Lewis was relieved when Clark and the rest of the party arrived on August 17th. Sacajawea recognized one of the girls as having been captured with her five years earlier at Three Forks, near present-day Bozeman, Montana. The other girl, Jumping Fish, had escaped while being taken to the Mandan Indian villages in North Dakota where Sacajawea was sold to Charbonneau. Even more amazing was the discovery that Chief Cameahwait was Sacajawea's brother! While Sacajawea had shown no emotion as they neared her homeland, she was very excited when she found both her friend and her brother. Sacajawea jumped up and ran to embrace Cameahwait, throwing a blanket over the two of them as she wept profusely.

Sacajawea was the only member of the party who could speak the Shoshone language, but it still took four people to converse. Captains Lewis or Clark would speak to Private Francois Labiche, who would translate it into French for Charbonneau to translate into Hidatsa for Sacajawea to translate into Shoshone. Thus, Sacajawea was the key to obtaining horses from the Shoshone Indians. Lewis was encouraged by the fact there were between 400 and 700 horses grazing around the camp. The survival of the Corps would depend on being able to obtain some of those horses.

View of the Lo Lo Peak area and the formidable mountains which loomed ahead. Near the present-day border of Idaho and Montana. POSTCARD FROM THE AUTHOR'S PRIVATE COLLECTION.

... "no easy route"...

"These guys grew up in the Appalachians, Daniel Boone and all those guys. That's what mountains were to them, and they hadn't seen anything like this. That's why I think Clark and Lewis both assumed they were going to go up this mountain, cross a ridge, and head down. They didn't comprehend that there were 200 more miles of impassable terrain."

EPISODE 16

A Big Disappointment

Chief Cameahwait drew a map in the dirt and made it clear there was no easy route across the Rocky Mountains. Lewis attempted to "*obtain what information I could with rispect to the country.*" Lewis had hoped the Lemhi River flowed through the mountains, but Cameahwait told him it flowed north for a half day's march before joining the Salmon River. Cameahwait told of "*vast mountains of rock eternally covered with snow through which the river passed, that the perpendicular and even jutting rocks so closely hemmed in the river that there was no possibilyte of passing along the shore; that the bed of the river was obstructed by sharp pointed rocks and the rapidity of the stream such that the whole surface of the river was beat into perfect foam as far as the eye could reach.*"

Cameahwait told Lewis he had never crossed the mountains, but "*that he had understood from the persed nosed* [Nez Perce] *Indians who inhabit this river below the rocky mountains that it ran a great way toward the setting sun and finally lost itself in a great lake of water which was illy taisted, and where the white men lived.*"

Lewis now had a pretty good idea about the drainage west of the Continental Divide. Cameahwait told Lewis the Nez Perce crossed the mountains every year to hunt buffalo in present-day Montana. Cameahwait said their route was to the north, "*but added that the road was a very bad one as he had been informed by them and that they had suffered excessively with hunger on the rout being obliged to subsist for many days on berries alone as there were no game in that part of the mountains which was broken rockey and so thickly covered with timber that they could scarcely pass.*" On August 21st the men awoke to find a quarter-inch of ice on jugs of water. Everyone was aware of the short time left to cross the Rocky Mountains.

It's NOT downhill all the way?

It appears Lewis and Clark were still in a state of denial. A water passage through the mountains was still a desperate dream they both wanted to realize if possible. Lewis traded a uniform coat, a pair of leggings, a few handkerchiefs, three knives, and some trinkets for three horses, "*the whole of which did not cost more than about 20$ in the U'States.*" Clark and eleven men then set out to explore the Salmon River to see if there was a possibility of going that route. But after a week, he knew the Indians hadn't lied. Clark sent a man with a note telling Lewis to buy more horses since the Salmon River was impassable. Today, the Salmon River is still known as the River of No Return.

"LEWIS AND CLARK MEETING INDIANS AT ROSS' HOLE," BY CHARLES M. RUSSELL

Russell memorializes the critical September 1805 meeting that first put the Expedition in touch with the Flatheads, or Salish, who would provide them with their horses for the critical next stage of the trip. The largest painting Russell ever did, the 12 foot by 25 foot mural hangs in the legislative chamber of the Montana State Capitol in Helena. Note again the primacy of the Indians in the narrative, with Lewis and Clark, with Sacajawea interpreting, in the background.

... relegating? ...

Ironically, amidst a culture accused often of relegating Indians and marginalizing them, Russell if anything "relegated" the white men of the Expedition in many of his paintings. Speaking of his most famous canvas, the magnificent mural "Lewis and Clark Meeting Indians at Ross' Hole," one historian noted, "By relegating Lewis and Clark to the quiet of the middle ground at right, Russell gives over the most important part of the picture space to Montana's original inhabitants. Nowhere else in the Capitol is the Indian presence in Montana so celebrated."

Meanwhile Lewis had, *"purchased five good horses of them very reasonably, or at least for about the value of six dollars a piece in merchandize."* While Clark was exploring the possibility of going down the Salmon River, Lewis used the horses, a mule, and some Shoshone women to carry their cargo the rest of the way from Camp Fortunate to Cameahwait's camp at Lemhi Pass where the journey through the mountains would begin.

A minor inconvenience?

On August 26th, Lewis wrote *"one of the women who had been assisting in the transportation of the baggage halted at a little run about a mile behind us... I enquired of Cameahwait the cause of her detention, and was informed by him in an unconcerned manner that she had halted to bring fourth a child... in about an hour the woman arrived with her newborn baby and passed us on her way to the camp."*

While still transporting their cargo, Charbonneau told Lewis he had learned the Indians were going to leave the next day to hunt buffalo — before Lewis could purchase the additional horses they would need. He was able to delay their departure and bought 22 more horses on August 28th. Clark hired an old Shoshone Indian called Toby to guide them over the mountains, and two days later the rest of the Shoshone Indians left to go hunt buffalo. The Corps reached the North Fork of the Salmon River on September 1st, and then traversed mountainsides so steep the horses slipped and slid down the slopes. Rain and snow fell, making the journey even more dangerous.

Is this the way to San Jose?

On September 4th, they met 400 Salish Indians (called Flatheads by Lewis and Clark) with 500 horses near present-day Sula, Montana. They bought 13 horses and exchanged 7 others. Toby then led the Corps down the East Fork of the Bitterroot River. When asked, Toby confessed he had no idea if the river joined the Columbia River (it does). The Expedition had traveled north along the Continental Divide and across trail-less mountains to get to Travelers Rest. Toby told the Captains of a trail from there east to the Great Falls that only took four days; the Corps circuitous route had taken 53 days.

The Corps spent a couple of days at Travelers Rest on Lolo Creek, ten miles southwest of present-day Missoula, Montana. While hunting, George Colter ran into three Nez Perce Indians and brought them back to Travelers Rest. One of them agreed to guide the Corps the rest of the way over the mountains, which, he said, was a six-day hike. However, the Nez Perce guide

... "the most terrible mountains" ...

"*They were up in the hillsides and it's rugged. It is nasty country. I can't even imagine people like you and me going up there with a backpack even and trying to get across it without using existing roads. It would be a real challenge. One of the horses that fell in the river had Clark's writing desk on it and broke it to smithereens. I always wondered what he did after that to write. How did he make his maps and everything?*"

abandoned them a day later. The Corps continued to follow an old trail that had been used by the Nez Perce since the 1730s. This trail is still visible today.

Travel was extremely difficult and, as Chief Cameahwait had said, there were virtually no animals to shoot and eat. On September 13th they reached Lolo Hot Springs and saw a bathing hole used by the Indians. They crossed the Bitterroot Mountains at Lolo Pass and began the journey down the Lochsa River, which joins the Clearwater River. The men were starving. The portable soup they had brought from St. Louis was rancid. Finally, on September 14th, they killed a horse to eat. It would not be the last time they had to do that.

Patrick Gass wrote, these are *"the most terrible mountains I ever beheld."* As bad as the journey had been up to that point, the worst was yet to come. The journey over those unknown, formidable snow clad mountains will be covered next episode.

OREGON HISTORICAL SOCIETY MUSEUM 3670.1

Captain Lewis's Branding Iron

About 4 x 5.5 inches and about 1-1/2 inches in depth, the branding iron carries the information "U. S. Capt. M. Lewis" at the top, with a large open rectangle below. The brackets on each side were probably attached to a short handle. The iron was primarily intended to brand trees, establishing the passage of the Corps. The open rectangle permitted other information, such as a date, to be added by carving. The branding iron was used to mark the grave of Sgt. Charles Floyd who died from a burst appendix in 1804, and may also have branded supply boxes and barrels at the outset of the journey. The horses left in the care of the Nez Perce Indians were branded in October 1805, possibly with this branding iron. Joseph Whitehouse wrote, "Got up our horses and cropped their fore mane, and branded them with a Stirrup Iron on the near fore Shoulder, So that we may know them again at our return."

The branding iron accompanied the Corps of Discovery to the mouth of the Columbia River, where it was used to brand trees and so mark the group's successful transcontinental trek. On the return trip in 1806, the iron was likely traded to Indians in the vicinity of Celilo Falls. The branding iron was found among rocks along the Columbia's north shore, west of The Dalles, in the early 1890s. It was given to Philip Jackson, publisher of the Oregon Journal, who donated it to the Oregon Historical Society in 1941.

EPISODE 17

The Worst Is Yet to Come

In this episode month, we continue the saga as the Corps of Discovery made their way across the Rocky Mountains. When Lewis and Clark learned there was no way across the mountains at Lemhi Pass, east of present-day Salmon, Idaho, the Shoshone Chief told of a trail north of there, used by the Nez Perce Indians to cross the mountains to hunt buffalo. With the help of Toby, an old Shoshone Indian, the Corps made their way to the east side of Lolo Pass, near present-day Missoula, Montana. This 150-mile journey, following the Continental Divide and down the Bitterroot River, took two weeks. The steep slopes and lack of a trail part of the way made it a difficult trip. However, anyone who thought the worst was over was in for a big surprise.

On September 11, 1805, when the Corps left the Bitterroot valley to climb 2,300 feet to reach Lolo Pass, they began the most difficult part of their 4,000-mile journey from St. Louis to the Pacific Ocean. A Nez Perce Indian had agreed to guide them the 160 miles over the mountains but abandoned them after just one day, leaving Old Toby, who had never crossed the mountains, to be their guide.

Much of the land the 33 Expedition members passed over remains unchanged today. Highway 12, across the Idaho panhandle, follows their route to some degree, but there is a Forest Service road that pretty much follows their actual route for most of the way from Lolo Pass to Orofino.

What's for dinner?

Finding enough deer and elk to feed the men had been difficult for many weeks. The portable soup brought from St. Louis was so rancid the men could eat only small portions. On September 14th, they were *"compelled to kill a Colt"* to keep from starving. Part of the horse was saved for breakfast and dinner the next day. Things would get worse.

Rather than following the river all the way, the Nez Perce trail followed the ridge tops. As a result, Toby made a couple wrong turns along the way. On September 15th, they left the valley floor and climbed 3,500 feet to reach the trail far above. At one especially steep section, several pack horses fell backwards and rolled 100 feet down onto the rocks. Up to a dozen men were needed to help those poor animals back up the hill. None of the horses died from the many falls, but the baggage they were carrying was damaged. Clark's portable writing desk was broken to pieces in one such accident.

After leaving the river, both water and game were scarce. Fortunately, they found snow banks up to three feet deep on some north facing slopes that could be melted to get water. The remainder of the first sacrificed horse was eaten for dinner that night, along with more putrid portable soup.

..."The want of provisions"...

"It was getting pretty bad by then. They had this stuff made up way back a year and a half before in St. Louis, just add water to make soup, and it was rancid. If they'd had anything else to eat they would've eaten it, but they couldn't even find chipmunks out there. This is out where nothing grows. If you don't pack your food with you, you die, and that's what Lewis and Clark were faced with. They had 33 men and nothing. So they ate their horses."

Turn up the heat!

Captain Clark woke up at 3am on September 16th to find it snowing. It continued all day, and by evening there was eight inches on the ground. This made a difficult situation almost impossible. Private Whitehouse wrote, "*Some of the men without socks raped rags on their feet...*" Following the trail was a challenge, and heavy wet snow falling off tree branches kept everyone soaked. Clark wrote, "*I have been wet and as cold in every part as I ever was in my life, indeed I was at one time fearfull my feet would freeze in the thin mockersons which I wore...*" A second horse was killed that night to feed the men.

Much time was lost when the men had to go searching for horses that wandered off each night. They couldn't afford to eat horses and lose them too. Snow continued the next day, but by evening it stopped and temperatures rose, melting the snow and making the trail muddy and slippery. That night, a third horse, "*being the most useless part of our Stock... fell a Prey to our appetites.*" Breakfast on September 18th finished that horse, and another horse wandered off not to be found. Morale was very low; years later, Clark wrote, "*The want of provisions together with the difficuely of passing these emence mountains dampened the Spirits of the party.*"

The end is near

Clark and a small party had gone ahead to seek food. On September 18th, Clark realized they had crossed the worst of the Rocky Mountains. He wrote, "*from the top of a high part of the mountain... I had a view of an emence Plain and Leavel Country to the S W. & West at a great distance.*" A lost Indian horse found grazing in a meadow became breakfast for Clark's party, with the remainder of the carcass hung in a tree for Lewis' party to find the following day.

The trail was terrible. Robert Frazier's horse fell off a steep precipice and rolled 300 feet down the drop-off into a creek. Fortunately, the horse missed the rocks and landed in a pool of water. After the heavy load of ammunition was taken off the horse, it "*arose to his feet & appeared to be but little injured, in 20 minutes he proceeded with his load.*"

Is there a doctor in the house?

On September 20th, Clark arrived at a Nez Perce village, east of present-day Orofino, Idaho. The warriors were away looking for enemy Indians, but the women gave Clark and his party all the dried salmon and boiled quamash (camas) roots they wanted. They ate too much and Clark wrote, "*I find myself verry unwell all the evening.*"

Dugout Canoes

The Indians showed the Corps members how to use hot coals and fire to help hollow out the canoes. It took ten days to build five canoes. They were notoriously hard to manage and unstable. It's a marvel that, fully laden with supplies and men, they stayed afloat, let alone made their way to the mouth of the Columbia. Even the Indians were skeptical, lining the banks at a hazardous river passage near today's The Dalles, waiting to salvage cargo and rescue drowning men. The canoeists and their primitive craft somehow survived that passage, and many others.

When Lewis and the rest of the men arrived two days later, Clark *"cautioned them of the Consequences of eating too much."* The next morning, Lewis and several men were very sick. Clark broke out the bottle of Dr. Rush's bilious pills, better known as "Thunderclappers." These pills, consisting mostly of chlorine and mercury compounds, did an excellent job of cleaning out their intestinal tracts, something Lewis and most of the men didn't need since they were sick with acute diarrhea for over a week. What made everyone so sick? Was it bad water, bacteria in the dried salmon, or the roots they ate? We'll never know.

Extreme hunger

The men managed to shoot some deer, but another perfectly good horse was sacrificed for a meal on October 2nd. A few days later, some of the men began buying dogs from the Indians to eat. Captain Clark wrote, *"all the Party have greatly the advantage of me, in as much as they all relish the flesh of the dogs."* The Nez Perce had many dogs, but since they never ate them, they disapproved.

The Nez Perce chief drew a map for Clark showing the rivers leading to the ocean. He indicated one place, present-day The Dalles, Oregon, might require portaging around the rapids. Everyone was excited at being able to build dugout canoes and ride the last 500 miles to the Pacific. They only had small axes, so it must have been difficult to fall the three- or four-foot diameter pine trees. The Indians showed them how to use hot coals and fire to help hollow out the canoes. It took ten days to build five canoes.

The Nez Perce had exceptionally nice horses. They were the only Indians to practice selective breeding, which had produced the Appaloosa. Since the Corps would not need their 38 remaining horses to get to the ocean, arrangements were made to have the Nez Perce take care of them until the following spring. Lewis branded each horse and cut off their manes. If the Corps failed to return, the horses would belong to the Indians.

Finally: Downhill all the way

On October 7th, the 33 members of the Expedition set off in their canoes down the Clearwater River. The canoes were packed full and took in water at many rapids while the men learned how to navigate them downriver. Sergeant Ordway described a near disaster a day later, *"One of the canoes Struck a rock in the middle of the rapid and Swang round and Struck another rock and cracked hir So that it filled with water. The waves roared over the rocks and Some of the men could not Swim. Their they Stayed in this doleful Situation until we unloaded one of the other canoes and went and released them."* Unlike the failed Iron Boat Experiment at Great Falls, pitch from the plentiful pine trees was available and used to repair the leaks in this canoe.

The Shoshone Indian guide, Old Toby, and his son disappeared on October 9th. The Nez Perce saw them running eastward toward Lolo Pass. Clark had not paid Toby, so he tried to get the Nez Perce chief to track them down. The chief told Clark not to bother since Toby would be robbed of anything he had as he passed through Nez Perce camps. In 1806, on their return trip, the captains were told Toby had taken two of the Expedition's horses as payment for his services. Toby was never seen or heard of again, but he most likely had saved the Corps from death by leading then to and through Lolo Pass.

Welcome to Washington

On October 10th, the Corps reached the confluence of the Clearwater and Snake Rivers at present-day Lewiston, Idaho. It took six more days to travel down the Snake River to reach the Columbia River at present-day Pasco, Washington. Private Whitehouse said the water flowed *"swifter than any horse could run."* Traveling with the current sure beat the months of rowing, poling, pulling, pushing, and carrying the boats up the mighty Missouri.

Even though the Snake River has been tamed with four dams in Washington, you can still get a feel of the canyon by driving south out of Kahlotus towards Pasco; take Route 263 down into Devil's Canyon. Stop at Windust Park, just downstream from Lower Monumental Dam, to fully appreciate the Snake River Canyon. Continue driving along the river until you come to Burr Canyon and return to the Pasco-Kahlotus Highway.

THE *Sea*

Native Americans fishing at Celilo Falls prior to the Falls being flooded in 1956 after construction of The Dalles Dam. U.S. Army Corps of Engineers.

... they reached Celilo Falls...

The Falls were the beginning of more than 50 river miles that also included the Short Narrows and the Long Narrows, which today we know jointly as The Dalles. This difficult passage through lava flows and columnar basalt ended with the Cascades of the Columbia. Moving quickly downstream in the autumn of 1805 — even though slowed by the portages — the Corps passed through this region approaching the Cascades of the Columbia in 13 days.

The Columbia River Plateau is formed by basalt flows, in present Washington, Oregon, and Idaho. Retreating glaciers of the last Ice Age left an ice dam trapping glacial melt water. This ice dam broke and re-formed as many as 40 times, releasing vast torrents of water westward with an estimated force 60 times that of the Amazon River.

EPISODE 18

Shooting the Rapids!

In October, 1805, after fighting their way up the Missouri River and across the Rocky Mountains, the Corps of Discovery must have been happy to float down the Snake River to present-day Pasco, Washington. Clark wrote the Columbia *"river is remarkably clear and crouded with salmon in many places... Salmon may be seen at the depth of 15 or 20 feet."*

Hot Dog!

Thinking they were diseased, the men were afraid to eat dead, spawned-out salmon lying along the shore, so they purchased 40 dogs as they began their journey down the Columbia. More than 250 dogs would be eaten during the journey. Lewis wrote that he preferred dog meat to lean venison or elk, but Clark wrote, *"I have not become reconciled to the taste of this animal."*

The abundant fish allowed for a dense population of Indians in permanent villages. It was a rare day that the Corps didn't see settlements while floating down the Columbia. There were no trees as far as the eye could see, so they had to purchase firewood from the Indians.

On October 22nd, they reached Celilo Falls, where the river was funneled through a series of drops totaling 38 feet. Indians were hired to help portage the cargo around the falls while the men rode their five dugout canoes down all but one of the drops. Shooting the rapids was a foolish thing to do, but Lewis and Clark were in a hurry to reach their goal and were reluctant to spend the time to portage around every rapid. There would be several more dangerous sections on the Columbia in the next 55 miles.

On October 24th they found nine miles of narrow channels with fast currents and eddies at The Dalles. Clark wrote, *"at this place the water of this great river is compressed into a Chanel between two rocks not exceeding forty five yards wide and continues for a ¼ of a mile when it again widens... The whole of the Current of this great river must at all Stages pass thro' this narrow chanel."* Clark was dismayed by *"the horrid appearance of this agitated gut Swelling, boiling & whorling in every direction."*

There was no easy portage, so the non-swimmers walked along the shore while the rest of the men shot the rapids. The Indians were astonished and lined up to watch the crazy white men drown themselves, undoubtedly waiting for the chance to help themselves to their equipment after the canoes capsized. Amazingly, all five canoes made it through without serious incident.

.... happy to float down ...

"*At first it wasn't exactly easy street. They weren't used to making dugout canoes. Their axes were crude for making boats. If the Indians hadn't shown them how it would have taken longer to come up with something resembling a boat. The hull was not shaped anything special. It was just a log floating down the river with men in it and a bunch of baggage. If it got a little bit off kilter, it turned over. They had a lot of trouble even getting down the Clearwater, until they got to the Snake. The boats would get hung up on sand bars and gravel bars and get cross-wise and lose their cargo or lose the men. One of the most amazing things to me was when they chose the people to go on this expedition, they didn't choose people who could swim. That was not a criteria. Half of them couldn't.*"

While visiting the many Indian villages, the men were exposed to a new problem. Clark wrote, "*The Flees which the party got on them at the upper & great falls, are very troublesom and dificuelt to get rid of, particularly as the me[n] have not a Change of Clothes to put on, they Strip off their Clothes and kill the flees, dureing which time they remain neckid.*"

The end is near

After passing Celilo Falls, Clark observed what he described as sea otters and seals. Since sea otters never enter fresh water, they were undoubtedly seals and sea lions. As the scorched, barren hills transitioned into moist, green tree- covered mountains, it began raining. Forty five miles below The Dalles, they reached "The Great Shute," now called Cascade Locks. After portaging around the cascades on November 2nd, they passed "Beaten Rock" (today's Beacon Rock) and camped at Rooster Rock. Clark noticed 9-inch tidal effects on the river at Rooster Rock, and 18 inches the next day.

On November 3rd, they passed the "*Quick Sand River*" (today's Sandy River) and camped on Government Island where I-205 now crosses the Columbia. Joseph Whitehouse wrote, "*we met Several Indians in a canoe who were going up the River. They Signed to us that in two Sleeps we Should See the Ocean vessels and white people.*"

On November 4th, they saw an Indian village on Sauvie Island, near St. Helens, with 25 houses built of straw and covered with bark. Clark noted he saw increasing amounts of "*uriopian*" goods: guns, powder flasks, copper and brass trinkets, and tailored clothes. John Ordway wrote, "*one of the Indians could talk & Speak Some words English such as curseing*" picked up from encounters with sailors. They camped near today's Ridgefield Wildlife Refuge where Clark wrote, "*I could not sleep for the noise kept by the Swans, geese... ducks.*" He added, "*they were emensely numerous and their noise horrid.*"

Urban sprawl – and an urban legend

On November 5th, they passed 14 wooden plank houses at the Cathlapotle village near Ridgefield, and another Cathlapotle village at the mouth of the Lewis River. Clark wrote the Lower Columbia region was "*certainly a fertill and handsom valley, at this time crowded with Indians.*" At the mouth of the Kalama River was an abandoned village. Capt. Clark called it "*Cath-la-haws Creek*" while Joseph Whitehouse wrote, "*we continued on & passed the Mouth of a River called by the Natives Calamus.*" In 1811, Gabriel Franchere wrote in his journal that the river and village was called "Thlakalamah." In the Cathlamet dialect of the Chinook language ,"Kalama" was the Indian word meaning "beautiful." Today, many people mistakenly believe the Kalama

This postcard, printed in 1913, looks upstream towards Pillar Rock, a basaltic column that extends from 50-foot deep water. Clark first saw the ocean from here, and wrote, "a remarkable rock about 50 feet high and about 20 feet Diameter is situated opposite our Camp about ½ a mile from Shore." In the late 19th century, the Army Corps of Engineers blasted the top off the rock in order to install a navigation beacon.

POSTCARD FROM THE AUTHOR'S PRIVATE COLLECTION.

Pillar Rock as it exists now, truncated to accommodate a navigation beacon.

River was named after John Kalama, a full-blooded Hawaiian who lived near the mouth of the river and worked for the Hudson Bay Company. However, since John didn't arrive until 1837, there is no connection. The Corps camped between Prescott and Rainier on November 5th, near where the Trojan Nuclear Power Plant was located.

On November 6th, the men saw abandoned villages on both sides of the Columbia near the mouth of the Cowlitz River. Clark wrote, "*The Coweliskee river is 150 yards wide, is deep, from Indian information navigable a very considerable distance for canoes.*" Lewis later said the principal village of the Skillutes was on the lower side of the Cowlitz a few miles from its entrance into the Columbia. They passed two lodges on the Oregon side across from Mt. Coffin, downstream from the present-day Lewis and Clark Bridge at Longview-Rainier. Clark described Mt. Coffin (named by Capt. George Vancouver's 1792 expedition) as "*a verry remarkable knob riseing from the edge of the water about 80 feet high*" (it was actually 240 feet tall). They camped that night near Cape Horn, east of Cathlamet.

The next morning the fog was so thick they could not see across the river, but they set out with great hopes of soon arriving at the ocean. They passed four large houses near Cathlamet. The houses were raised off the ground, with beds four feet above the floor. They saw another seven houses at a village near Skamokawa, and when the fog lifted, they could hear the roar of the ocean.

Ocian in view! O! the joy

At last, on Nov. 7, 1805, near Pillar Rock (12 miles downriver from Skamokawa), Clark wrote, "*we are in view of the opening of the ocian, which Creates great joy.*" The men saw a magnificent vista – the river had widened to about five miles and they could see that the sky met the water at the horizon where the Columbia flowed into the Pacific Ocean between Point Adams and Cape Disappointment. But they were still more than 20 miles from the actual coastline, and getting there was going to be a most miserable journey.

... two hours in a row without rain ...

"If you read the journals, there's about four or five days in a row where he's trying to say the same thing in different words. It is really a desperate time; they're up against this steep cliff and the rocks are coming down on them and the tides are bringing these big logs in. They're soaked and they've got nothing. They have no food. The best they can do is shoot a duck or catch a fish or something — but you've got 33 men that are dying of cold and starvation. And I think that Clark, what he was writing there was desperate, and truly from the heart."

EPISODE 19

Ocian in View!

When the Corps of Discovery camped near Cape Horn, east of Cathlamet, on November 6, 1805, they knew they were getting close to the ocean. The next morning the fog was so thick they couldn't see across the river, but they set out with great hopes of soon arriving at their destination. After they passed an Indian village west of Skamokawa, the fog lifted and they heard the roar of the ocean. That night at Pillar Rock, Clark wrote, "*we are in view of the opening of the ocian, which Creates great joy.*" In a second notebook, Clark wrote, "*Great joy in camp we are in View of the Ocian, this great Pacific Octean which we have So long anxious to See.*"

So near and yet so far

When Clark wrote "*ocian in view*" on November 7, 1805, they were still 20 miles from the actual coastline. The Corps thought they would reach the coast the next afternoon since 35-mile days had been typical as they traveled down the mighty Columbia the previous three weeks. However, these last 20 miles would prove to be the most miserable part of the entire journey.

The next day, a severe storm halted all progress and Clark wrote, "*we are all wet and disagreeable, as we have been for Several days past, and our present Situation a verry disagreeable one in as much; as we have not leavel land Sufficient for an encampment and for our baggage to lie Cleare of the tide, the High hills jutting in So Close and Steep that we cannot retreat back, and the water of the river too Salt to be used, added to this the waves are increasing to Such a hight that we cannot move from this place, in this Situation we are compelled to form our Camp between the hite of the Ebb and flood tides, and rase our baggage on logs.*"

The shoreline was covered with large drift logs. Clark wrote that some were upwards of 200 feet long and 7 feet in diameter. The waves and high tides tossed the logs, threatening to crush the men and their canoes. In an effort to save their canoes, they used large rocks to submerge them. It was impossible to proceed until the storms let up.

When it rains it pours

Journal entries for the next two weeks reinforced how miserable their situation was. A series of winter storms had them pinned down east of the present-day Astoria-Megler bridge at what Clark called "*this dismal nitich.*" Every time they tried to round Point Distress (today's Point Ellice), huge waves turned them back. The men were trapped for six days along the narrow shore

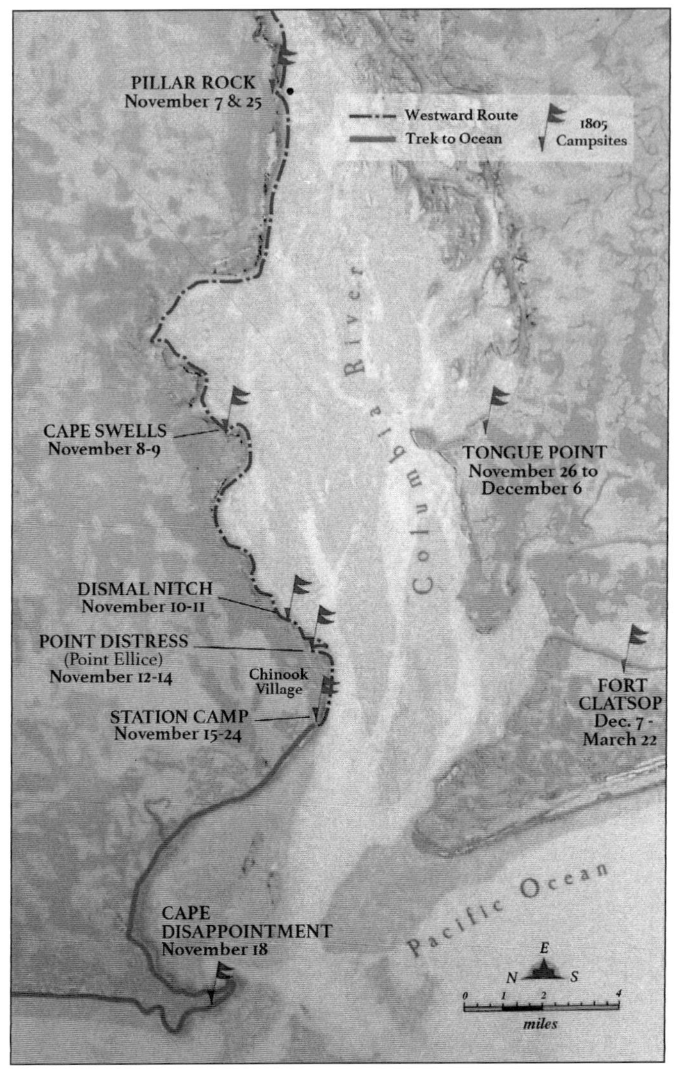

This map showing the mouth of the Columbia was created for the National Park Service in 2005 as part of an informational display at the Megler rest stop.

... a missed opportunity...

"These guys had to really have had it. To be totally done in. It was a cakewalk to go down and see the ocean. And the ones that never saw the ocean at Long Beach and never went down to Cannon Beach to see the whale, never saw the Pacific coast at all. I mean, what an empty feeling that would be. Or, how tired and sick of it all you really might have been."

as rocks pelted down from the steep bank above. Clark wrote *"every man as wet as water could make them."* In 11 days, they experienced no more than two hours in a row without rain.

Their buffalo, elk and deer skin clothing was soaked and rotting away, leaving some men nearly naked. Efforts to find elk or deer failed. They supplemented the few birds they shot with pounded fish purchased at Celilo Falls and with fresh fish they caught. During one stormy day, a boat of "*War-ci-a-cum*" Indians stopped by to trade with them. After buying some fish, Clark wrote, *"the Indians left us and Crossed the river which is about 5 miles wide through the highest Sees I ever Saw a Small vestle ride… Certain it is they are the best canoe navigators I ever Saw."* The Indians had learned to make exceptional boats, whereas Lewis and Clark's dugout canoes bobbed around like corks.

Desperate times

On November 12th, Clark wrote, *"It would be distressing to a feeling person to See our Situation at this time"* and, *"our Situation is dangerous."* Two days later, in desperation, Lewis decided to set out by land to try to get around Point Distress and see if there were any trading ships there. But the river became calm during a slack tide and he was able to get a canoe around the point. The next day, Clark was able to take the rest of the men around Point Distress where they camped on a sandy beach. They were now in plain view of the ocean and could see the waves and surf crashing across the Columbia bar. Lewis returned two days later and reported there were no ships or white men in the area.

Just a little farther

On November 17th, Clark invited *"all the men who wished to See more of the main Ocean to… Set out with me."* Only 11 men took him up on his offer. Surprisingly, over half the men who had just traveled more than 4,000 miles had no desire to go the last few miles to see the ocean! At Cape Disappointment, Clark wrote they looked *"with estonishment the high waves dashing against the rocks & the emence ocian."* Today's north jetty has allowed sand to accrete in that area, so you will not see what Clark saw when you go there.

During their three-day journey to Cape Disappointment and the 9-mile walk along the beach to present-day Long Beach, the men saw a dolphin, a flounder, and a 10-foot sturgeon washed up on the shore. They also saw whale bones. And, Sgt. Ordway wrote they saw *"a verry large turkey buzzard"* which was shot in the name of science so Clark could better examine it. That "buzzard" was a California condor – one of many the expedition would see on their journey. It had a 9-foot wing span and was almost 4 feet in length.

... the local Indians ...

Historians estimate that Lewis and Clark interacted with between 50 and 70 Native American tribes, including the Nez Perce, Mandans, Shoshones, and the Sioux. The captains followed Jefferson's instructions to gather all the information they could — their cultures, military strength, lifestyles, social codes, and customs. Interactions with the Clatsop and Chinook Indians were especially important to their stay at the mouth of the Columbia. In 1805 they found some 400 Clatsops living in several villages on the southern side of the Columbia River and south down the Pacific Coast to Tillamook Head. The Chinooks lived on the northern banks of the Columbia and on the Pacific Coast, while the Nehalem, the northernmost band of the Tillamook, lived on the Oregon coast at Tillamook Head south to Kilchis Point. They are described by historians as shrewd traders and masterful canoe builders. Despite complaints of pilfering and other nuisances, the captains felt they had been treated with "*extrodeanary friendship.*"

It had been two weeks since Clark first saw the ocean. And while they had made it around Point Distress and established Station Camp near an abandoned Chinook Indian village, the weather was still miserable. On November 22, Clark wrote *"waves brakeing with great violence against the Shore throwing the water into our Camp &c. all wet and Confind to our Shelters."* On November 23, 1805, Clark wrote, *"I marked my name the Day of the month & year on a Beech* [alder] *trees… Capt Lewis Branded his and the men all marked their names on trees about the Camp."* They had seen names of sailors from trading ships carved on other trees.

All in favor say 'Aye'

On November 24th, each member of the expedition, including Sacajawea and Clark's slave, York, was asked for their opinion of where to spend the winter. The north shore was out of the question due to the constant storms and lack of elk. A few deer had been shot, but the men needed elk to replenish their clothing. The Clatsop Indians told them there were lots of elk on the south side of the river. So the choice was whether to cross the river or go back upriver to spend the winter near The Dalles.

Wintering near the mouth of the Columbia had advantages — the weather would be milder, there was elk to eat, they could boil seawater to make salt to preserve the elk meat, and if a trading ship arrived they would be able to replenish their supplies. Everyone except Sacajawea's husband, Charbonneau, voted, and all but one person voted to cross over to the Oregon shore to spend the winter.

The next day they headed back upriver to cross at Pillar Rock where the river is narrower. Nobody was interested in crossing the five miles of open water at Station Camp! Lewis went ahead, seeking a place to spend the winter. Meanwhile, storms returned and pinned Clark's party down near Tongue Point. Clark wrote, *"O how Tremendious is the day."* The wind *"blew with Such violence that I expected every moment to See trees taken up by the roots, maney were blown down. O! how disagreeable is our situation dureing this dreadfull weather."* Clark carved his name on a tree, *"Capt. William Clark December 3rd 1805. By Land. U. States in 1804 & 1805."*

Hunters managed to shoot some elk, the first since crossing the Rocky mountains. Clark became worried about Lewis and his detachment since they had been gone for five days; Clark feared they'd had an accident. A day later, Lewis returned and said he had found a good place to spend the winter. Two days

Ocean in View! O! the joy.

... the first writer to challenge the belief ...

"*As far as the mouth of the river goes, there wasn't anything in the journals to speak of, just these things that Rex quotes. That's why all the other interpretive books, they just kind of glossed over it, didn't even have them come down the Washington side. So, it was really a wake-up moment when I got to this point in the story. If I hadn't read Rex's book, I would be very disappointed in how little was here. Rex captures what is the most dismal, miserable, challenging time of the whole journey. And it was right here at the mouth of the Columbia.*"

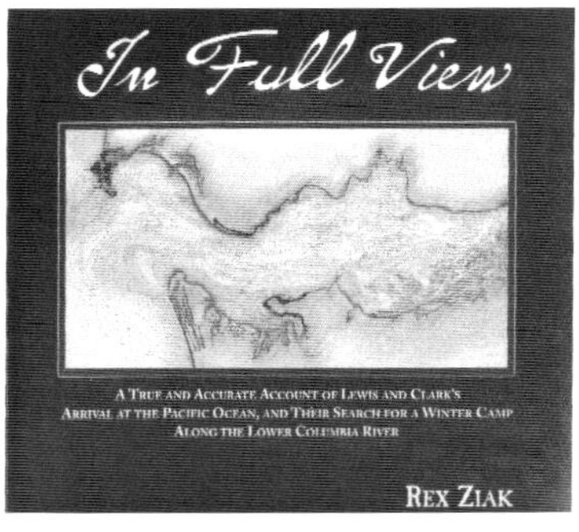

Rex Ziak's first book, "In Full View," published in 2002, revolutionized Lewis and Clark scholarship.

later, after the storms passed, everyone traveled to the site where Fort Clatsop would be built – Clark wrote it was a *"most eligible situation."* It was located on a bluff above the Netal River, about 7 miles inland from the ocean. Plans were drawn up for a log fort and construction began on December 10. The men moved into their new winter quarters on Christmas Day in 1805.

Clark's Controversial Words

NOTHING WRITTEN BY LEWIS AND CLARK has caused as much controversy as Clark's famous words, *"Ocian in view! O! the joy."* Virtually all historians believe Clark was mistaken, and that what he actually saw was just Grays Bay and the Columbia River estuary. After all, when he wrote those famous words at Pillar Rock, they were still 20 miles from the ocean. But, how could Clark have made such a big mistake and not correct it later? And, just how did so many people come to doubt what Clark wrote?

It wasn't until 1904, almost a hundred years after Lewis and Clark completed their journey, that the first complete edition of their journals was edited and published by Reuben Thwaites. Thwaites, who never visited the mouth of the Columbia, wrote a footnote stating *"The ocean could not possibly be seen from this point."* This statement was based on information from a friend who had gone to Pillar Rock and reported back that the view of the ocean was blocked by Point Adams west of Astoria. Historians reading that footnote assumed Thwaites was correct, and repeated it in their own books.

It is doubtful if Thwaites took into consideration the South Jetty at the mouth of the Columbia that was completed in 1895. This four-mile long jetty extended northwest out into the ocean from Point Adams. Sand immediately began to accumulate around the jetty as it was built, and by 1900 there was a forest growing on the hundreds of acres of newly accreted land at the northwest tip of Oregon, blocking the view where the ocean had been just 15 years earlier. While it was indeed impossible to see the ocean from Pillar Rock in 1904, in 1805 there had been a view of 6 degrees between Point Adams and Cape Disappointment. Thus, it is quite likely Clark saw where the sky met the water – but was it the ocean?

The curvature of the earth is about 8-inches per mile. Thus, the surface of the flat ocean is 13-feet below the horizon when looking west along the surface of Columbia River from Pillar Rock. Surface water elevations at Pillar Rock vary from three to six feet above sea level. If Clark was sitting in his canoe, his eyes would have been another three feet higher. And, if he

Rex Ziak presenting his Lewis and Clark story in 2004.

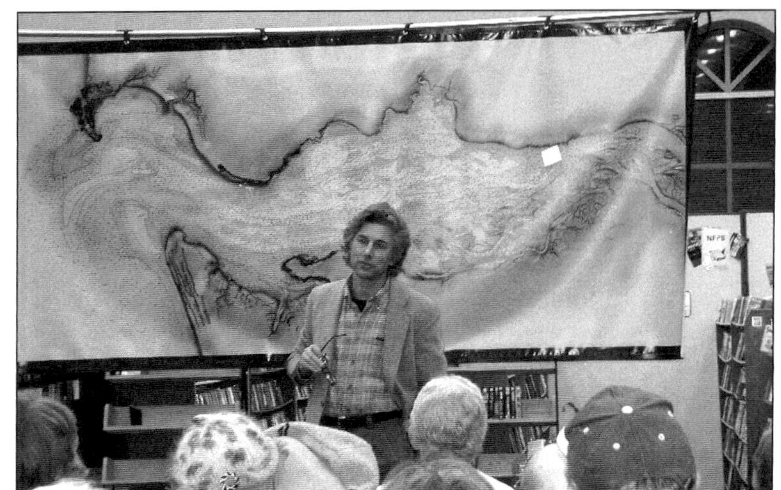

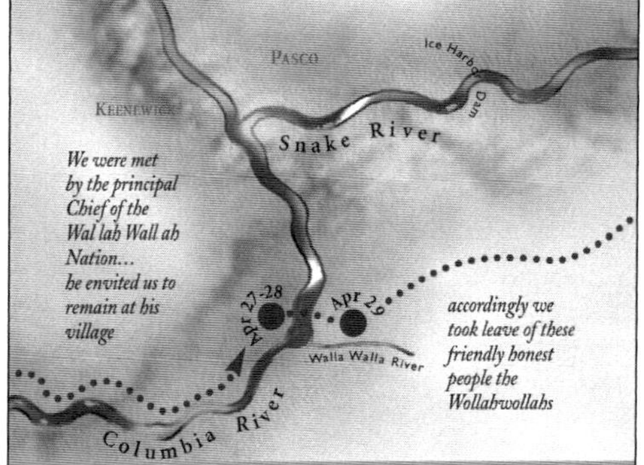
Pasco
Snake River
We were met by the principal Chief of the Wal lah Wall ah Nation... he envited us to remain at his village
Apr 27-28
Apr 29
Walla Walla River
accordingly we took leave of these friendly honest people the Wollahwollahs
Columbia River

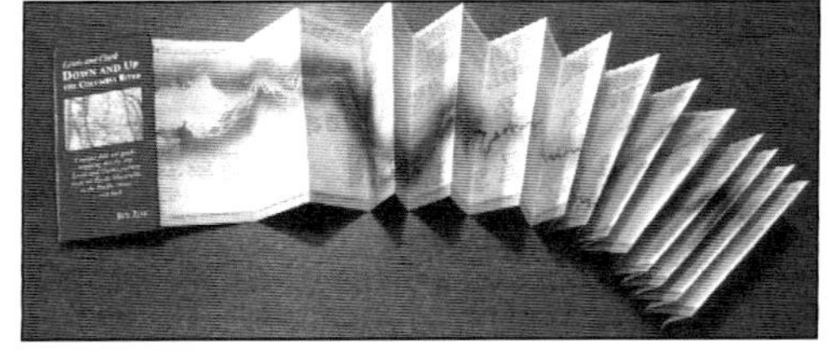

After publishing his landmark book, "In Full View," in 2002, Ziak led tours of key sites near the mouth of the Columbia River. As the bus unloaded near Dismal Nictch, Ziak busied himself, using chalk to draw a long map on the sidewalk. The map, showing the Columbia River drainage from Idaho to the Pacific, was the basis of his talk. He described the Corps making their way from the Bitterroot Mountains to within five miles of the Pacific Ocean in a month, then taking another full month to reach the ocean and crossing the Columbia to where Fort Clatsop was built. That chalk-drawn map led to Ziak's second book, "Lewis and Clark Down and Up the Columbia River," a foldout map that captures his sidewalk presentation. He describes "Down and Up" as a one-page book that took a dozen years to research.

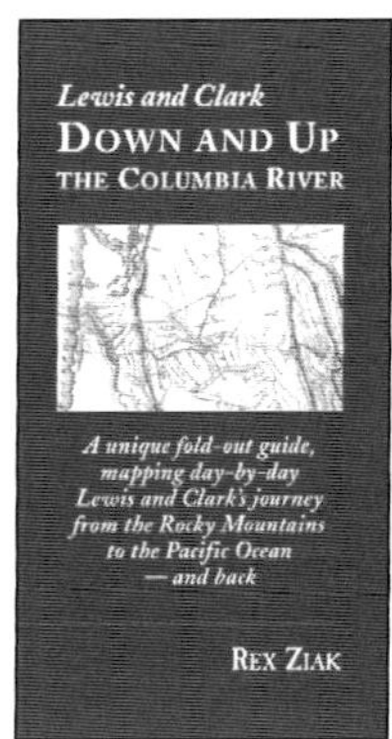
Lewis and Clark
DOWN AND UP
THE COLUMBIA RIVER
A unique fold-out guide, mapping day-by-day Lewis and Clark's journey from the Rocky Mountains to the Pacific Ocean — and back
REX ZIAK

stood to look at the mouth of the river through his telescope, he would have been six feet above the water. Thus, in theory, Clark could have seen the tops of waves and swells in the ocean. The Expedition experienced a series of winter storms that November, with storm swells likely upwards of 10 feet high. Also, since the ocean's waves came further into the mouth of the Columbia before the jetties changed things, it seems likely Clark did see the ocean's waves from Pillar Rock.

It is interesting to note that none of the Corps' other journal writers mentioned seeing the ocean on November 7th. Many historians cite this as evidence that Clark was mistaken. However, Clark had made other mistakes in his journal entries, but he always corrected them at a later date when he realized he'd been wrong. In this case, he had several opportunities to correct the record when they returned to Pillar Rock at a later date. But no such correction was made.

In fact, on December 1st, after going back upstream to Pillar Rock to cross over to Tongue Point on the Oregon side, Clark wrote, *"The Sea which is imedeately in front roars like a repeeted roling thunder and have rored in that way ever Since our arrival in its borders which is now 24 Days Since we arrived in Sight of the Great Western Ocian."* Clark had to do some calculating to be able to say it had been 24 days since he had first seen the ocean; 24 days earlier had been November 7th. Thus, even after he had been to the ocean and back to Pillar Rock, Clark made no corrections – in fact, he affirmed his original statements of November 7th.

In 2002, Rex Ziak of Naselle wrote an outstanding book that local history buffs will enjoy. His book, *In Full View*, focuses on just one month of the Corps' journey and is the most insightful work about the Lewis and Clark Expedition I have found. It is likely no other living person knows as much as Mr. Ziak about what the Corps of Discovery experienced between November 7 and December 7, 1805.

Ziak was the first writer to challenge the belief that Clark had been wrong about seeing the ocean on November 7. After reading his book, I find it hard to imagine anyone not agreeing with him. Rex grew up in the Naselle area and spent 10 years researching his book, retracing their footsteps during the same nasty weather the Corps experienced.

Ziak used an extremely detailed navigation chart, showing the mouth of the Columbia River 20 years before the south jetty was built, to help the reader understand the daily events. The map shows that when Captain Clark was at Pillar Rock, he had a clear view of the opening where the Columbia River flows into the Pacific Ocean.

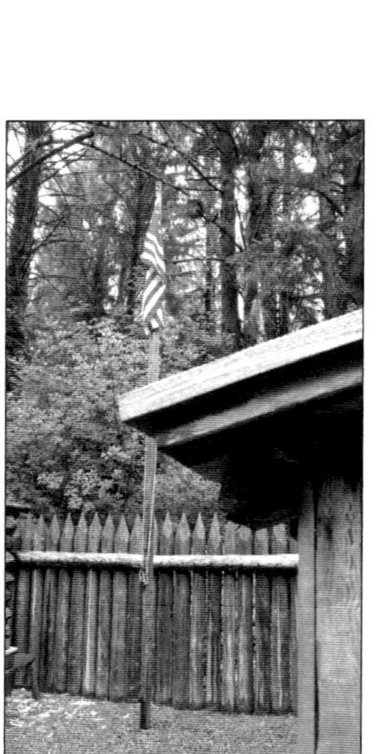

Lewis and Clark re-enactors play an important role at today's re-built Fort Clatsop replica. The metal container the re-enactor is holding contains char-cloth.

EPISODE 20

Fort Clatsop, Winter 1805–6, Snuggly Fixed, Pass the Salt

As we learned in the last episode, the Expedition spent a miserable two weeks trying to reach the Pacific Ocean following the sighting of the mouth of the Columbia River from Pilar Rock on November 7, 1805. After deciding to spend the winter on the south side of the river, they loaded their canoes and went back upstream where the river was narrower and crossed over to Tongue Point. Lewis and a couple of men went ahead seeking a place to spend the winter. For the next five days, storms returned, pinning down Clark's party and preventing Lewis' party from returning. Clark became worried about Lewis, fearing he'd had an accident. A day later, Lewis returned and reported he'd found a good place to spend the winter.

The Corps constructed a log fort under a canopy of old-growth Sitka spruce somewhere near today's reconstructed Fort Clatsop. The fort was on a bluff on the west side of the Netal river, southwest of present-day Astoria and about 7-miles from the ocean. While it was a dark, damp and mossy setting, it provided protection from the gale force winds and crashing waves that the Corps had experienced in November as they made their way along the north shore of the river to reach the Pacific Ocean.

Nothing but the best-est

Plans were drawn up for a log fort and construction began on December 10th. The first priority was building a meat house since "*all our last Supply of Elk has Spoiled in the repeeted rains which has been fallen ever Since our arrival at this place, and for a long time before*." It only took two weeks to build Fort Clatsop with the "*Streightest & most butifullest logs*."

During that time, it rained continuously. It snowed and hailed. Lightning and strong winds added to the dismal conditions. Clark described December 16th as "*Certainly one of the worst days that ever was!*" During their four-month stay at the mouth of the Columbia River, only twelve days were without rain. Finding enough dry wood for their fires was a constant challenge.

A Christmas to remember

On December 25th, Joseph Whitehouse wrote, "*We saluted our officers, by each of our party firing off his gun at day break in honor of the day (Christmass)*." Sergeant Ordway wrote, "*They divided out the last of their tobacco among the men that used and the rest they gave each a Silk handkerchief, as a Christmas gift, to keep us*

THE SALT MAKERS," BY JOHN F. CLYMER, 1975.

From a National Park Service sign in Seaside, Oregon. After the Lewis and Clark Expedition was established at Fort Clatsop, members of the group camped here from January 2 to February 21, 1806. The explorers conveniently found stone to build an oven, wood to burn, fresh water to drink, elk to hunt, and seawater to boil, having "... a good concentration of salt."

... five men hiked to the ocean ...

The Corps had run out of salt for seasoning food, and, perhaps more important, for preserving meat. Preserving meat was critical for the Corps. The elk meat harvested near Clatsop was lean and tasteless. If it spoiled it made the corpsmen sick. And they hoped to lay in a good supply of salted meat for the journey home. To make salt, the Corps needed rocks to build a furnace, wood to burn, and ocean water to boil. They also needed fresh water and game to survive their sojourn at the coast. The party found a site 15 miles southwest of Fort Clatsop. Five men traveled to the beach site, built the camp and set five kettles to boiling 24 hours a day. According to their records, they set out from Fort Clatsop on Dec. 28, 1805, and left the camp Feb. 20, 1806, with 3.5 bushels or about 28 gallons of salt.

in remembrence of it as we have no ardent Spirits, but are all in good health which we esteem more than all the ardent Spirits in the world. We have nothing to eat but poore Elk meat and no Salt to Season that with." Clark wrote they had "*a bad Christmas diner*" consisting of unsalted, spoiled lean elk meat, spoiled pounded fish purchased two months earlier at Celilo Falls, and a few roots.

Itching to see Santa?

Everyone had moved into the still uncompleted fort by Christmas Day, and Clark wrote they were "*Snugly fixed.*" Sleeping under a roof must have been a great relief, but they still had to deal with the fleas "*that torment us in such a manner as to deprive us of half the nights Sleep.*" Sergeant Gass wrote, "*the ticks, flies and other insects are in abundance, which appears to us very extraordinary at this season of the year, in a latitude so far north.*"

In their rush to build the fort, the men had neglected to build chimneys for the fireplaces. Whitehouse wrote, "*We found that our huts smoaked occasion'd by the hard wind; & find that we cannot live in them without building Chimneys.*" A day later, Whitehouse wrote the chimneys were "*completed, & found our huts comfortable & without smoak.*"

On December 28th, five men hiked to the ocean, near present-day Seaside, to set up a salt making operation. A week later, Lewis wrote that two of the men brought back "*a specemine of the salt of about a gallon, we found it excellent, fine, strong, & white; this was a great treat to myself and most of the party.*" Prior to that, much of their meat had spoiled in the warm and damp conditions. In seven weeks, enough sea water was boiled to extract 3-1/2 bushels gallons of salt, most of which was used to preserve meat for their return trip the next spring. While at Fort Clatsop, 131 elk and 20 deer were killed.

New Year's Day of 1806 was welcomed with a volley of gunshots, "*the only mark of rispect which we had it in our power to pay this selebrated day.*" The men were, almost certainly, already making plans for the trip back to St. Louis in spring. But first, they had to survive a soggy winter.

This photo, taken less than two weeks before the Fort Clatsop replica burned down in 2005, shows smoke coming out of the chimney in the middle room. On that day, a re-enactor was demonstrating how the Corpsmen made candles by heating a kettle of tallow over a fire. This is probably where the fire started that destroyed the fort.

This photo shows a "fireplace" in the rooms at Fort Clatsop, which was simply an open fire built on a stone slab. There was no enclosed chimney; the smoke rose in the room to escape through a hole cut in the roof.

Fort Clatsop Replica

THE FIRST FORT CLATSOP replica, built in 1955, burned down on October 3, 2005. Rather than rush to rebuild it in time for the 2005 Bicentennial events, it was decided to take a little time and try to do it right. In the 50 years since it was built, historians had learned more about the fort and knew the 1955 reconstruction was not as accurate as it might have been. However, while the replacement fort would end up incorporating some of the new knowledge to better reflect how the original fort may have been constructed, a decision was made to build the new fort on the old 1955 foundation even though evidence indicated the original fort was "U" shaped rather than made up of two parallel structures facing each other, open at both ends.

In late 2005, after the charred debris was cleared, excavations were made under the replica fort in search of evidence of the Lewis and Clark expedition. In three weeks of digging and sifting, the only things found were pieces of broken glass and pottery made after Lewis and Clark's visit. A blue bead found was believed to have been made after 1850. Previous excavations in the area also failed to turn up any evidence of elk or deer bones, the Corps' garbage pit, or a latrine pit (which could be identified by high levels of mercury from Dr. Rush's infamous "Thunderclappers" used to treat many Corps members' illnesses). Thus, there still is no clear evidence of where the original fort was located.

The replacement fort was constructed indoors at the Clatsop County Fairgrounds so that visitors could watch as it was built. The reconstruction began on December 10, 2005, which happened to be 200 years to the day after Lewis and Clark started construction of the original fort. After the new replica fort was built, it was disassembled and treated with a wood preservative and then rebuilt at the Fort Clatsop site.

The view from Ecola Point on the trail across Tillamook Head, north of Cannon Beach, along the route that Capt. Clark and 12 men (plus Sacajawea) took in January 1806 to get to the whale that had washed ashore near Cannon Beach. Clark wrote that he saw "inoumerable rocks of emence Sise out at a distance from the Shore and against which the Seas brak with great force gives this Coast a most romantic appearance."

EPISODE 21

Great Treats: Sea Salt and Blubber

In late December of 1805, five men hiked from Fort Clatsop to the ocean, near present-day Seaside, to set up a salt-making operation. A week later, Capt. Lewis wrote that two men brought back *"a specemine of the salt of about a gallon"* that was used to make their lean and often spoiled elk meat somewhat palatable. However, the salt makers also brought back a sample of blubber from a beached whale that Indians had found near present-day Cannon Beach. Sgt. Ordway wrote, *"we mix it with our poor elk meat & find it eats very well."* Capt. Clark decided to set out the following day in an attempt to purchase some more blubber.

Sacajawea wanted to go along. When Clark said no, *"She observed that She had traveled a long way with us to See the great waters, and that now that monstrous fish was also to be Seen, She thought it verry hard that She Could not be permitted to see either (She had never yet been to the Ocian)."* Clark agreed to her request.

On January 6th, Clark and 12 men, plus Sacajawea and her French husband Charbonneau, hiked to the salt makers' camp where they hired an Indian to guide them to the whale. They walked along the beach until they reached an *"emence mountain the top of which was obscured in the clouds."* They camped high on the bluff, and the next day climbed to the top of Cape Falcon where Clark saw *"the grandest and most pleasing prospects which my eyes ever surveyed, in my frount a boundless Ocean."*

Anyone who has ever hiked across Tillamook Head can appreciate what the men saw as they looked south towards Cannon Beach. Clark wrote, *"inoumerable rocks of emence Sise out at a distance from the Shore and against which the Seas brak with great force gives this Coast a most romantic appearance."*

When they reached the whale, all that was left was the 105-foot long skeleton. The local Indians had completely stripped it. Clark was able to purchase only 300 pounds of blubber and a few gallons of whale oil, but he was grateful to get anything to add to the lean elk they ate virtually every meal. Prior to that, an occasional dog purchased from the Clatsop Indians was the only thing that made meals something to look forward to.

The daily journal entries illustrate how boring their days were in January and February. Lewis repeatedly wrote, *"Nothing worthy of notice occured today."* The men spent the winter preserving meat by smoking and drying. They also chopped firewood, repaired their weapons, dressed elk and deer skins, made clothes, etc. They made 338 pairs of moccasins. In addition, they traded with the Indians. Typically, the Indians wanted more than the men

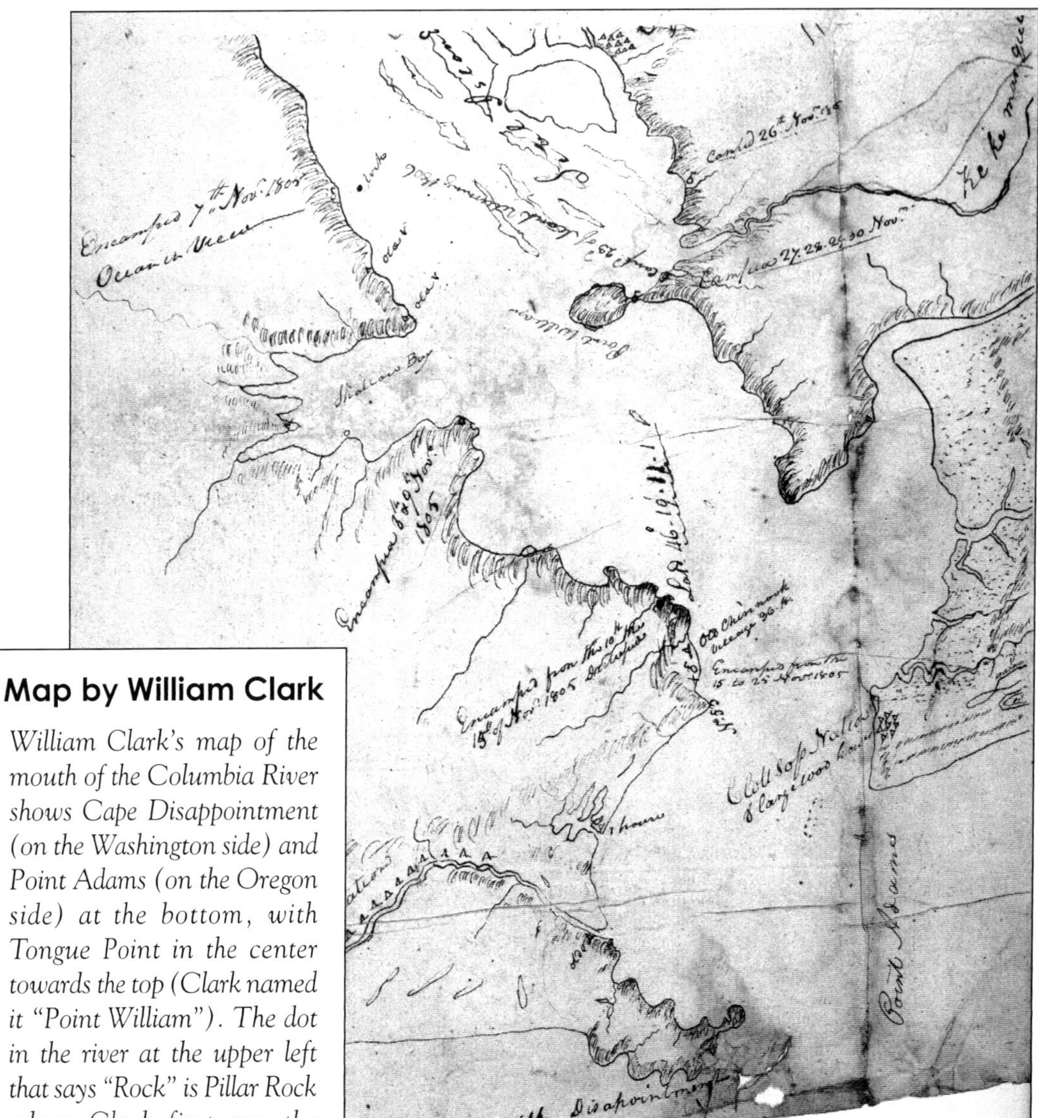

Map by William Clark

William Clark's map of the mouth of the Columbia River shows Cape Disappointment (on the Washington side) and Point Adams (on the Oregon side) at the bottom, with Tongue Point in the center towards the top (Clark named it "Point William"). The dot in the river at the upper left that says "Rock" is Pillar Rock where Clark first saw the ocean on Nov. 7, 1805... see the notation to the left of that dot that reads "Encampment 7th Nov. 1805 - Ocian in View." Additional notations along the Washington shore show where they camped on Nov. 8–9 and Nov. 10–15, and Nov. 15 – 25... then, up by Tongue Point, Clark shows where they camped on Nov. 26, and then from Nov. 27 – 30.

had to offer, but after a lot of haggling, a trade was often agreed to. Undoubtedly, the silk handkerchiefs the men had received at Christmas were traded to Indian maidens who were willing to sell their favors to the men.

Don't forget your flu shot

The weather at Fort Clatsop was miserable. Everything was wet, and it snowed several nights in December, January, and February. On January 26th, they awoke to eight inches of snow on the ground. The men were not eating a balanced diet and were prone to illness. The men experienced colds, boils, the flu, strained muscles, and venereal disease. On Feb. 22, Lewis wrote, *"we have not had as many Sick at any one time Since we left"* St. Louis in 1804. Ordway wrote, *"Six of the party are now Sick I think that I and three others have the Enfluenzey."*

Everyone in the Corps of Discovery had a job. Lewis was the leader; others were hunters, carpenters, woodsmen and blacksmiths. William Clark was the mapmaker. Captains Lewis and Clark spent much of their time at their writing desks. Lewis described and drew sketches of the dozens of plants and animals they had seen. Ten plants, two fish, eleven birds, and eleven mammals were new to science. He also recorded details about each Indian tribe they had met along the trail, describing their culture, language, and what they ate.

Mapmaker, Mapmaker, make me a map...

Clark spent his spare time drawing charts and maps. Even though the Corps had failed to find a water route across the continent, the maps Clark would create were probably the most important thing that came from the journey. When the Expedition left St. Louis in 1804, Clark took along the best maps available. He had a large comprehensive map, drafted by Nicholas King in 1803, with a longitude and latitude grid accurately showing the course of the lower Missouri River, as well as the Pacific Coast. Clark's job was to fill in the blank area in the middle of that map.

During the winter of 1805 at Fort Clatsop, Clark consolidated his field notes covering their journey west from North Dakota to the Pacific Ocean. He made a series of small maps that were used to create a large detailed map after the journey was over. Clark kept detailed field notes in his journal showing courses and distances traveled each day. If Clark assumed cartographers would use his painstakingly recorded traverse to create accurate maps after the journey was completed, he was wrong.

Amazingly, nobody had ever used Clark's field notes to create a set of maps. For almost 200 years, those field notes were ignored until a resident of Vancouver, Washington, published a three-volume set of Lewis and Clark Trail Maps. Martin Plamondon

Lewis and Clark National Historical Park, National Park Service

Wintering Over

Historical re-enactors participate in regular demonstrations and special occasions at Fort Clatsop, Lewis and Clark National Historical Park. During the Bicentennial Commemoration, for example, park visitors exchanged Christmas gifts with Expedition "members."

II, a descendent of Southwest Washington pioneer Simon Plamondon, worked for 30 years to create a set of more than 500 maps covering the entire 7,400-mile route Lewis and Clark took.

Sadly, Plamondon died just before his third and final volume was published in 2004. Plamondon's maps make the Expedition journals come to life in a way previously impossible. Captain Clark would have loved these maps. More on this in Episode 32.

Would the Corpsmen recognize today's Fort Clatsop?

MARTIN PLAMONDON'S THIRD VOLUME of his Trail Maps, published in 2004, challenges several assumptions about the expedition in the Pacific Northwest. One example is his drawing of Fort Clatsop that is significantly different from the 1955 reconstruction that burned down in October 2005, and was rebuilt a year later using the same 1955 layout. Rather than two rows of rooms (three rooms in one row and four rooms in the other), separated by a 20-foot wide parade ground with a gate at each end, Plamondon thought the fort was actually U-shaped and consisted of three rows of connected rooms, with a walled stockade that extended out from the open end.

In 2005, before Fort Clatsop burned down, Scott Stonum, Fort Clatsop's resource management chief, agreed the 50-year old layout might have been inaccurate. "We do not claim that the fort replica is an exact replica," he said. The 1955 fort reconstruction was based on a preliminary design Captain Clark drew, whereas Plamondon's drawing was based on the journal entries by three of the men who built the original fort. The best description was recorded by Pvt. Joseph Whitehouse, but the 1955 replica builders did not have access to Whitehouse's writings since his journal was not discovered until 1966.

On December 11, 1805, Whitehouse wrote "*We raised one line of our huts today.*" This line probably formed the bottom end of the "U" and contained three rooms, one of which was the smokehouse. On December 13th, Sgt. John Ordway wrote "*we raised another line of our huts and began the last line of our huts forming three sides of a square and 7 rooms 16 by 18 feet large. the other square we intend to picket and have gates at the two corners, so as to have a defensive fort.*" The next day, Whitehouse wrote "*We finished raising the line of huts, & began to cover one of them, which Our officers intend for a Meat house &ca.*" Whitehouse also wrote that "*Fort Clatsop lay a small distance back, from the West bank of* [the Netul] *River. The fort was built in the form of an oblong Square, & the front of it facing the River, was picketed in, & had a Gate on the North & one on the South side of it.*"

THE

Return

of small fish which now begin to run and are taken in great quantities in the Columbia R. about 40 miles above us by means of skiming or scooping nets. on this page I have drawn the likeness of them as large as life; it as perfect as I can make it with my pen and will serve to give a general idea of the fish. the rays of the fins are boney but not sharp tho' somewhat pointed. the small fin on the back next to the tail has no rays of bone being a thin membranous pellicle. the fins next to the gills have eleven rays each. those of the abdomen have eight each, those of the pinnaeani are 20 and 2 haff formed in front. that of the back has eleven rays. all the fins are of a white colour. the back is of a bleuish duskey colour and that of the the lower part of the sides and belley is of a silve-ry white. no spots on any part. the first bone of the gills next behid the eye is of a bleuis cast, and the second of a light goald colour nearly white. the puple of the eye is black and the iris of a silver white. the under jaw exceeds the uper; and the mouth opens to great extent, folding like that of the herring. it has no teeth. the abdomen is obtuse and smooth; in this differing from the herring, ~~shad~~ anchovey &c of the Malacapterygious Order & Class Clupea

Captain Meriwether Lewis's eulachon sketch made on Feb. 24, 1806. "I think them superior to any fish I ever tasted, even more delicate and lussious than the white fish of the lakes which have heretofore formed my standard of excellence among the fishes."

EPISODE 22

Smelt Dip

On Feb. 24, while still at Fort Clatsop, the Corps obtained some smelt from Chief Comowooll and a dozen members of the Clatsop Indians. In 1806 Lewis wrote that smelt were *"a species of small fish which now begin to run, and are taken in great quantities in the Columbia R. about 40 miles above us by means of skiming or scooping nets. On this page I have drawn the likeness of them as large as life... the scales of this little fish are so small and thin that without minute inspection you would suppose they to have none. I find them best when cooked in Indian stile, which is by roasting a number of them together on a wooden spit without any previous preparation whatever."* The greasy little fish were a favorite of the Corps.

Homeward Bound!

While everyone was anxious to leave wet and dreary Fort Clatsop, they knew it would be impossible to cross the Rocky Mountains until the passes were clear of snow. If they started too soon, they would have to survive in a land where elk and deer were non-existent, and firewood was unavailable. Lewis wrote, *"two handkercheifs would now contain all the small articles of merchandize which we possess."* Clark wrote, *"On this stock we have wholy to depend for the purchase of horses and such portion of our subsistence from the Indians as it will be in our powers to obtain."*

Earlier in 1806, Meriwether Lewis and William Clark had decided to wait until April 1 to begin their journey home. The Corps of Discovery hoped a trading ship might arrive before they left the mouth of the Columbia. President Jefferson had recognized it might be "imprudent to hazard a return" by land, so he gave Lewis a letter of credit to purchase passage home on a trading ship, or to purchase supplies for the journey home overland. Unfortunately, no ships visited during the four months the Corps was at the mouth of the Columbia.

If the Corps hadn't taken so long to get around the Great Falls in Montana or across the Rocky Mountains in 1805, they would almost certainly have found a trading ship waiting for them at the mouth of the Columbia. Captain Samuel Hill and his ship, the Lydia, had departed Boston in August 1804, and were at the mouth of the Columbia in November, 1805. However, the Lydia left shortly before Lewis and Clark arrived in mid-November.

Decisions, Decisions...

On March 14, 1806, the Clatsop Indians told Clark that the Makah Indians, who lived on the Olympic Peninsula, reported four trading ships were visiting them. Thus, it is strange that

... they purchased wapato and a dog ...

Wapato grew abundantly and was eaten by many Native American tribes throughout Washington and Oregon. Often known as the "Indian Potato," the tubers were widely traded and given to the Expedition during times of food scarcity. Often, along the middle and lower Columbia, families owned patches of wapato, and camped beside these sites during harvesting season. Sauvie Island, in Multnomah County, Oregon, was named "Wappetoe Island" by Lewis and Clark. On March 29, 1806, Clark recorded how the women harvested wapato:

> *"by getting into the water, Sometimes to their necks holding by a Small canoe and with their feet loosen the wappato or bulb of the root from the bottom from the Fibers, and it imedeately rises to the top of the water, they Collect & throw them into the Canoe, those deep roots are the largest and best roots."*

Lewis and Clark decided not to wait for a ship to visit the mouth of the Columbia. But low morale among the men and a fear storms might delay their departure worried them. Food was becoming scarce at Fort Clatsop. The Corps had killed most of the elk, and those remaining were moving to higher ground now that winter was over. Many of the men were ill from the constant exposure to the cold rain and poor diet. So they decided to leave a week early, on March 23. But before leaving, they needed to obtain two more canoes.

The End Justifies the Means

Lewis's dress uniform jacket was traded for one canoe, but when attempts to buy another canoe failed, Lewis and Clark did something they had vowed never to do: They decided to steal a canoe from the Indians. They justified it by the fact some Clatsop Indians stole six elk killed by the Corps earlier that winter. When the owner of the canoe confronted the Corps a day after they left Fort Clatsop, demanding the return of his canoe, the 32 riflemen were able to convince him to accept a dressed elk hide in trade.

Home For Sale – Cheap!

Lewis and Clark gave Fort Clatsop and all the contents to Chief Coboway. He would live in the fort for several years, and in 1899 his grandson was able to point out where it had been located. Copies of a letter were given to various Indian chiefs, listing all the men and the purpose of the Expedition along with a map showing their route from St. Louis to the Pacific. The hope was that a visiting trading ship might obtain one of these letters and take it back to President Jefferson. Unfortunately, the ship that had been anchored at the mouth of the Columbia in November 1805, just before Lewis and Clark arrived, returned soon after they left in 1806. Indians gave the letter to Captain Hill when the Lydia sailed to China, eventually arriving at Philadelphia in January 1807 where the letter was forwarded to President Jefferson. However, Lewis and Clark had safely returned to St. Louis four months before the letter arrived. Still, if they had met some misfortune, Jefferson would have learned they had at least reached the Pacific Ocean.

Slow Going

On March 24th, they purchased wapato and a dog at an Indian village, near present-day Knappa, Oregon, to feed to the sickest men. They camped opposite present-day Skamokawa that night, and opposite present-day Cathlamet on March 25th. On March 26th, they camped on Fisher Island, downstream from present-day Longview, adjacent to Willow Grove. All winter long, the Expedition had been buying fish and wapato roots at high prices

Cape Horn and Cigar Rock. As they headed home, the Expedition members enjoyed re-visiting landmarks noted on their trip downriver. The Corps of Discovery had camped near Cape Horn, east of Camas, on their way to the Pacific Ocean on Nov. 2, 1805.

Postcard from the author's private collection.

from the Clatsop Indians. As they headed up the Columbia, they soon realized the prices were lower as they went upstream, due to eliminating the middlemen.

On March 27th, the Expedition stopped at a Skillute village downstream from present-day Rainier, where the Indians welcomed the men and gave them all the sturgeon, camas and wappato they could eat. Two miles further, they passed the mouth of the Coweliskee River (present-day Cowlitz River). Clark wrote, "*we Saw Several fishing camps of the Skillutes on both Sides of the Columbia, and also on both Sides of this river. The principal village of the Skil-lutes is Situated on the lower Side of the Cow-e-lis-kee river a fiew miles from it's enterance into the Columbia. those people are Said to be noumerous, in their dress, habits, manners and Language they differ but little from the Clatsops, Chinooks &c.*"

Lewis wrote, "*The Coweliskee is 150 yards wide, is deep and from indian Information navigable a very considerable distance for canoes. it discharges itself into the Columbia about three miles above a remarkable high rocky nole which is situated on the N. side of the river by which it is washed on the South side and is separated from the Northern hills of the river by a wide bottom of several miles to which it is united.*" The "*rocky nole*" Lewis described was Mount Coffin, a 225-foot tall basaltic column that was an Indian burial ground and historic landmark. Sadly, a Portland sand and gravel company leveled the rock in the early 20th century. In 1954, Weyerhaeuser Company purchased the land to build a chlorine plant.

Wapato Island

They camped somewhere between present-day Goble and the site of the decommissioned Trojan nuclear plant on March 27th. Then, on March 28th, they camped on Deer Island after spending all day repairing their canoes and hunting deer. On March 29th, they reached Wapato Island (present-day Sauvie Island), across from the Lewis River. In 1806, there were more people living on that island than there are today. This was where much of the wapato was grown. In fact, you can still see large patches of wapato in lakes and marshes on Sauvie Island.

Future Metropolis

They then crossed the river to the Cathlapotle village near the mouth of the Lewis River and bought 12 dogs and more wapato. They camped near present-day Ridgefield that night. The next night, they camped downstream of today's I-5 bridge near Vancouver. Lewis wrote, "*I took a walk of a few miles through the prarie... this valley would be copetent to the mantainance of 40 or 50 thousand souls if properly cultivated and is indeed the only desireable situation for a settlement which I have seen on the West side of the Rocky mountains.*" The timber growing in the flat bottomland

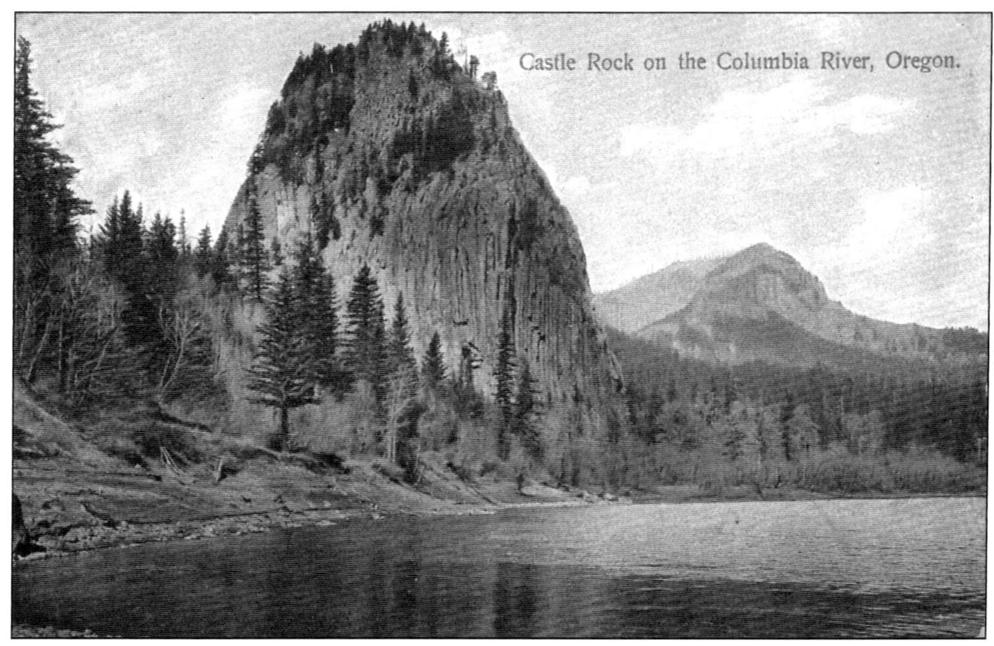

Beacon Rock, on the Washington side of the river, is now a state park and recreation area. On their way downriver, Lewis and Clark had noted tidal action and movement at the rock, indicating they were nearing the ocean, or at least its tidewater reach.

POSTCARD FROM THE AUTHOR'S PRIVATE COLLECTION

was abundant and impressive; Clark described a fallen fir tree measuring 318 feet long and just three feet in diameter near the Sandy River.

The Corps spent a week east of the Washougal River (which they named Seal River due to the abundance of seals at its mouth). Many Indians were visiting the area and reported a great scarcity of food upstream since the spring salmon run was not expected for another month. Clark wrote, "*this information gives us much uneasiness with respect to our future means of subsistence*." Thus, they decided to stay there until they had obtained enough meat to get to the Nez Perce lands.

"Lost" River

Several men were sent to explore the Quicksand River (present-day Sandy River). Based on the lay of the land, Clark knew there had to be another river that emptied into the south side of the Columbia. Since islands hid the mouth of the present-day Willamette River, the Corps had missed it going down and then back up the Columbia. Local Indians told Clark about the river (they called it the Multnomah River), and he hired a guide to show him where it was. Clark explored 10 miles up the river, to present-day northwest Portland.

Amateur Magician

While in an Indian lodge, Clark offered several things in exchange for some wapato. The Indians refused to trade with him, so Clark resorted to showing off his technology. He threw a piece of fuse-cord in the fire, which sizzled and burned like gunpowder. At the same time, he used a hidden magnet to make the needle of his compass spin rapidly. As they begged him to put out the bad fire, it quit burning by itself. The Indians gave him a basket of wapato, thinking he was "Big Medicine." They were terrified of the white explorer. Clark paid for the wapato and left.

Windsurfing, Anyone?

On April 6th, the journey resumed up the Columbia. Violent winds blowing through the Columbia Gorge halted progress several times, but by April 9th they reached the Cascades of the Columbia, near present-day Bonneville Dam. They noticed the water level at 700-foot tall Beacon Rock was 12-feet higher than it had been the previous November. This was interpreted to mean the snow on the east side of the Cascades was rapidly melting, and gave the Corps reason to hope they might find the Rocky Mountain passes to be snow-free when they got there. That would prove to be wishful thinking!

The Newfoundland Dog was the first animal to be commemorated on a postage stamp by any country. In 1894, Newfoundland issued a half-cent stamp showing the head of a Newfoundland dog. In 1930, they issued a 14-cent stamp honoring their namesake dog.

EPISODE 23

Homeward Bound, Still! What's the Holdup?

Newfoundland Dogs

WHILE PREPARING FOR THE EXPEDITION in 1803, Meriwether Lewis paid $20 for a *"dogg of the newfoundland breed."* Lewis failed to write about his reasons for buying this particular breed of dog, but I believe it was no accident. Lewis knew his men would be traveling on water most of the journey, and that many were not good swimmers. They needed a lifeguard.

Newfoundland dogs are web-footed and have natural life-saving instincts, so Lewis may have bought his dog with the idea it might save someone who fell overboard. Fishermen on the island of Newfoundland used them as water rescue dogs more than 1,000 years ago. They are big – over two feet tall and weigh up to 150 pounds. They are larger than a St. Bernard and share a tendency to slobber profusely. They were used for draft work, such as helping pull in fishermen's nets. Newfoundland dogs almost became extinct, and today the breed owes its existence to a single stud dog that lived 100 years ago.

Scannon, Seamon, or Seaman?

Until 1987, every book about Lewis and Clark referred to Lewis's dog as "Scannon." In 1984, while examining one of Clark's maps, a historian noticed that a creek near Missoula Montana was named "Seaman's Creek." Since there was nobody associated with the Corps of Discovery named Seaman, and since they were 700 miles from any ocean, it seemed odd. Whenever the Corps named a geographical feature, they usually picked a name of someone involved with the Expedition (such as Sacajawea's River) or that reflected the particular landmark (such as Milk River). It turned out historians had mistakenly interpreted the dog's name in the hard-to-decipher journals as "Scannon" while, in fact, the name on the map was correct: "Seaman." Sgt. John Ordway's journal also verified the dog was named Seaman — Ordway wrote it as "Seamon."

No official records exist as to the fate of Seaman. He was last mentioned in the journals on July 15, 1806, two months before the journey ended in St. Louis. Some people have speculated that the men got so desperately hungry they ate him, but that seems very unlikely. Others think he may have died or wandered off, never to be found. If anything like that had happened to Seaman, it seems almost certain one of the men would have recorded it in their journal. In all probability, Seaman returned to St. Louis and stayed with Lewis until either he or Lewis died (more on that in a future Dispatch). Newfoundland dogs typically live only 8–10 years, and very few of them walk 4,000 miles across the continent!

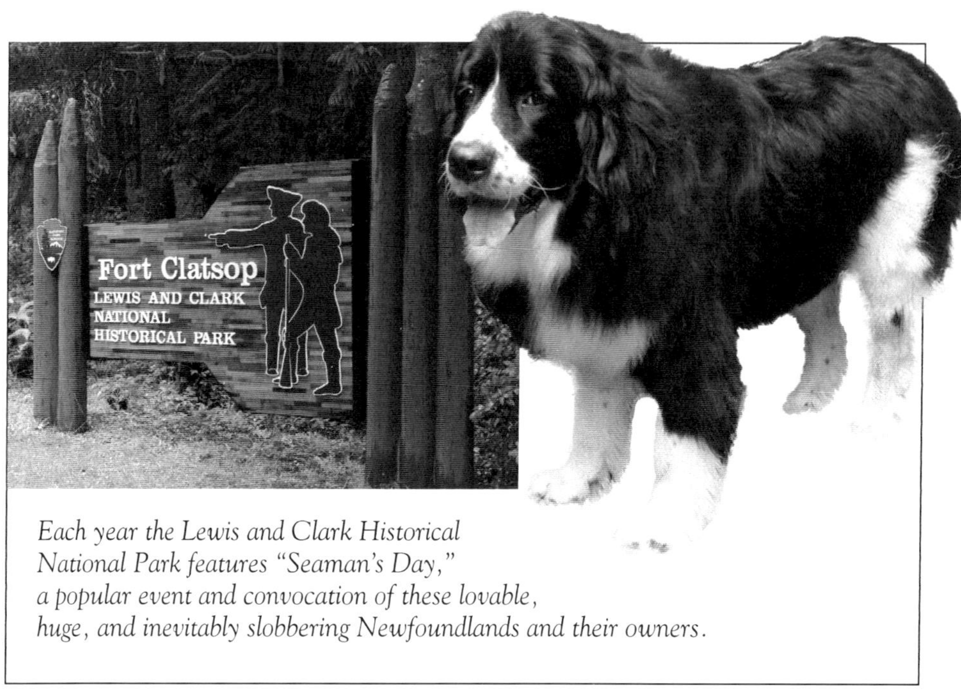

Each year the Lewis and Clark Historical National Park features "Seaman's Day," a popular event and convocation of these lovable, huge, and inevitably slobbering Newfoundlands and their owners.

While anxious to return home, the Corps spent the first nine days of April 1806 camped near Washougal, across from the Sandy River. Local Indians told them people were starving upstream since the spring run of salmon had not yet arrived. So, the Corps spent the time hunting and stockpiling meat to make the journey to the Nez Perce villages on the Clearwater River, where they had left their horses the previous fall.

Upon resuming their journey, they found it very tough going due to the high water and fast current. Rapids they had easily passed through in October 1805 were now impossible to traverse. They had to unload all their baggage and carry it around the rapids while the men tried to pull the five empty canoes upstream with ropes. One canoe got crosswise and was swept away. The four remaining canoes were unable to carry all the baggage, so Lewis bought two more from the Indians.

Doggone!

On April 11th, some Indians stole Seaman, Captain Lewis's black Newfoundland dog. Lewis wrote, "*I... sent three men in pursuit of the thieves with orders if they made the least resistence or difficulty in surrendering the dog to fire on them.*" He got his dog back. Lewis described this particular band of Indians as "*the greates thieves and scoundrels we have met with.*"

By April 15th, it was evident they would need horses to continue upstream. Attempts to buy some from three Indian villages failed because the Corps had nothing of value that they were willing to trade. Finally, Clark crossed the river and obtained 12 horses, and another six two days later. On April 18th, they reached a point where the two largest canoes could go no further, so the canoes were cut up for firewood. They needed more horses and, reluctantly, traded two large kettles for four more horses. Lewis was furious when one of the horses wandered away that night after one of the men failed to picket it.

The Indians caught the first salmon of the long-awaited spring run on April 19th. However, it would be a while before the Indians had enough to sell to the Corps of Discovery. Meanwhile, Lewis was becoming very mad at the Indians for the daily loss of goods. Six tomahawks, a knife, and two spoons were stolen on April 20th. And horses started to disappear. Charbonneau lost three horses in two days. Three more were purchased, and one was found and returned by an honest Indian.

On April 28th, Clark traded his sword for a "*very elegant*" white horse. He was also told about an overland shortcut they could take from Pasco to Lewiston. Food was becoming a real problem, but since their supply of trade goods was almost gone, the

Indians would not give them any food. Clark started trading medical treatments for food. His reputation was well known from his having provided similar treatments on the journey down the river the previous fall.

Abandon ship

On April 30th, they sold their remaining canoes and set off overland with 23 horses. A Walula Indian caught up with them and delivered a steel trap he had found near his village that one of the men had forgotten. The steel trap was a very valuable item, and based on all the other things that had been stolen from the Corps, it was remarkable that it was returned.

By May 4th, the Corps had reached the Snake River and a Nez Perce village. A day later, they reached the Clearwater River. A Nez Perce man brought two lead powder canisters his dog dug up from one of the supply caches the Corps had dug the previous year. The Indians had dug another cache to store the remaining material, but some saddles and other things were missing.

I don't want to hear it

On May 7th, the Indians told the Corps the Rocky Mountains would be impassible until June. That was not something they wanted to believe. Everyone wanted to get back to St. Louis! They found Chief Twisted Hair and arranged to get their horses back. Then, on May 10th, they awoke to find eight inches of fresh snow on the ground. Maybe the Indians were right after all? On May 15th, they decided to build camps and wait for the snow in the passes to melt. The men were encouraged to partake in contests of strength with the Indians to keep from getting too out of shape. The upcoming journey over the Rockies would be a real hardship, especially if the men sat around very long doing nothing.

With their supply of meat exhausted, they had a choice – eat roots and dried fish provided by the Indians, or eat horses. Everyone remembered how sick the party had become when eating roots and fish the previous year, so horse sounded pretty good. Even though the Nez Perce were appalled, they provided the horses the men needed. Some men ate the roots, but several got sick again. Some men cut the buttons off their uniforms to trade for food.

Big Medicine

In addition, Clark continued his practice of trading medical treatment for food. On May 24th, a Nez Perce chief who had not had the use of his arms or legs for three years was brought to

Captain Clark. He had no idea what was wrong, but gave the Indian a painkiller and tried to give him a sweat bath. The man was too stove up to sit upright inside the sweat house, so Clark had the Indians dig out the floor so he could get inside. Four days later, the Indian could move his arms and sit up unaided. On May 30th, he could move his legs and on June 8th he was able to stand up. No wonder the Indians thought Clark was big medicine!

Hit the road, Jack

By May 31st, the Corps had 65 horses and were anxious to leave. The Nez Perce recently had sent messengers across the mountains to visit the Flat Heads in Montana. When they returned on June 3rd, they said the passes were still full of snow and the Corps should wait another two weeks. The men decided to wait another week, but ended up waiting until June 15th to begin their assault on the Rockies. Surely, the passes would be clear of snow by then? We shall see.

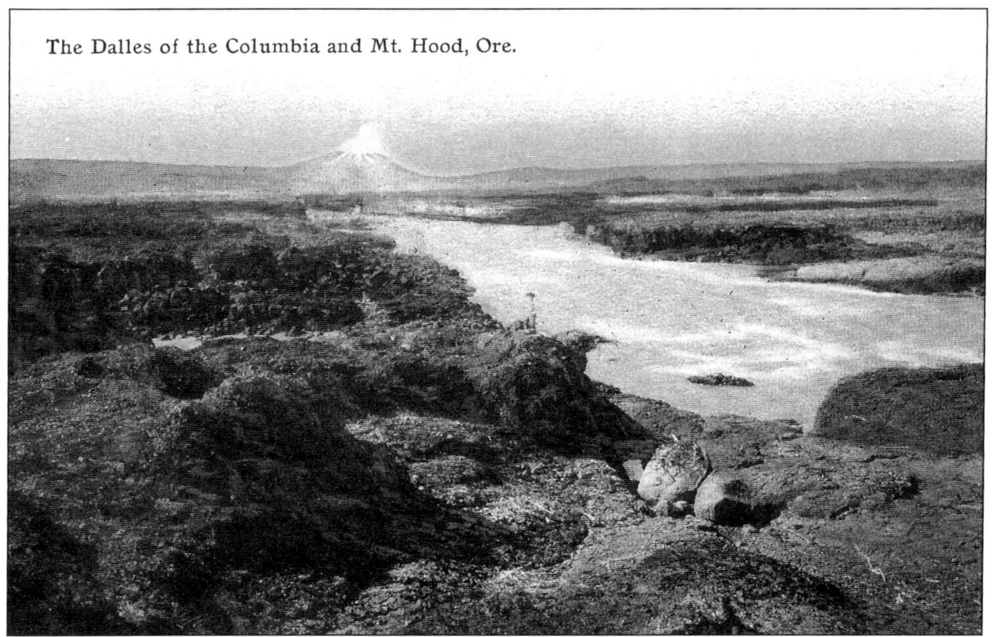

The Dalles of the Columbia and Mt. Hood, Ore.

Anxious to escape the dismally-wet Fort Clatsop, the Expedition met frustration on the "dry side" of the Cascade Mountains. They were eager to give up their canoes for horses.

POSTCARD FROM THE AUTHOR'S PRIVATE COLLECTION.

EPISODE 24

Chomping at the Bit Backfires!

As described in the last episode, the Corps was anxious to start their homeward journey after spending more than four months at the mouth of the Columbia. While they knew snow in the Rocky Mountains would be a major obstacle and, thus, planned to leave on April 1, 1806, they left two weeks early, hoping to escape the dismally wet conditions at Fort Clatsop. That was a mistake, since the spring salmon run they had counted on was late and, therefore, no fish were available from the Indians at The Dalles. The men spent two weeks camped across from the Sandy River to obtain enough meat to make the trip to the Nez Perce villages in Idaho.

Anyone got a snowplow?

When they reached the Nez Perce villages in early May, they were pleased to find their horses still there. However, the Indians told them it would be at least a month before they could cross the pass due to deep snow. So the next six weeks were spent waiting. Everyone was concerned about the delay, since they wanted to get back to St. Louis that year, and a long delay might mean having to spend another winter at Fort Mandan in North Dakota.

On the road again!

Finally, on June 15, they started the dreaded journey across the Rockies. The Indians told them it was still too early, but as Lewis wrote, "*every body seems anxious to be in motion.*" Clark wrote, "*I Shudder with the expectation with great dificuelties in passing those Mountains.*" They knew it could take a week to make the crossing. If the snow still covered everything, there would be no grass for the 65 horses, and without the horses they were doomed. A day later, as the horses grazed in a meadow surrounded by snow five feet deep, they realized they had left too soon. Still, they proceeded on another day and found the snow was ten feet deep and the trail was buried.

Benumbed and bewildered

Lewis wrote, "*here was winter with all it's rigors; the air was cold, my hands and feet were benumbed. We knew that it would require five days to reach… Colt Creek… short of that point we could not hope for any food for our horses as the whole was covered many feet deep in snow. If we proceeded and should get bewildered in these mountains the certainity was that we should loose our horses and… we should be so fortunate to escape with life.*"

… in an overhead cache …

The Expedition learned the technique of "caching" excess gear and supplies from the French Canadian "engages," (hired hands), many of whom they'd met and engaged, along with Charbonneau, at the Mandan Villages. Pierre Cruzatte was often given the responsibility of directing the work. Typically, caches were underground, beginning with a hole around two feet in diameter, which was systematically widened and deepened, then filled with heavy baggage and excess supplies to be picked up later. Unfortunately, for some unknown reason the structures didn't all meet Cruzatte's assurances. The cache at the mouth of the Marias River collapsed, ruining most of the contents, which included souvenir furs belonging to Lewis and some of the men, as well as many other personal possessions. The cache at the upper portage camp at the Falls of the Missouri was damaged by spring floodwaters that destroyed all of the plant specimens Lewis had collected between Fort Mandan and the Great Falls.

Decision time

That same day, Lewis wrote, "*we therefore came to the resolution to return with our horses while they were yet strong and in good order and indevour to… procure an Indian to conduct us over the snowey mountains… knowing from the appearance of the snows that if we remained until it had desolved sufficiently for us to follow the road that we should not be enabled to return to the United States within this season.*" Thus, they began a "retrograde march," after placing most of their supplies in an overhead cache made of poles hung between trees. The only things left to trade with the Indians were their guns. A week later, under promise of two rifles, some Nez Perce guides were hired and the journey began again, three months after leaving Fort Clatsop.

Early Fourth of July

On June 25, Lewis wrote, "*the Indians entertained us with seting the fir trees on fire. They have a great number of dry lims near their bodies which when set on fire creates a very suddon and immence blaze from the bottom to top of those tall trees… This exhibition reminded me of a display of fireworks. The natives told us that their object…was to bring fair weather for our journey.*"

Adieu to the snow

The Indians knew where to find meadows on south-facing slopes that would be clear of snow and thus provide new-grown grass for the horses. While the snow was still many feet deep, it was solid enough for horses to walk on without sinking in more than a few inches most of the time. However, once in a while the snow would not support a horse and it would sink in to its belly. Finally, on June 29, they "*bid adieu to the snow,*" and a day later reached Lolo Hot Springs. The men spent the next two days relaxing and recovering from the hard journey.

Divide and conquer

Before leaving Fort Clatsop, Lewis and Clark had made plans for the return trip. They wanted to explore different routes, so on July 3 the party split up. Captain Clark, along with Sacajawea and most of the party, went up the Bitterroot River, back to Camp Fortunate where they had found Sacajawea's tribe the previous year. However, this time nobody was to be found, since the Indians had gone east to hunt buffalo.

Sgt. Ordway "caches" in

Clark's group continued down the Jefferson River until reaching Three Forks on July 13. At that point, Sgt. Ordway and a detachment recovered the canoes they had cached the previous year and went down the Missouri River to Great Falls. There they would retrieve the material cached in 1805, and then continue on down the Missouri to meet up with Captain Lewis.

Clark mosies to Bozeman…

Clark took the rest of the party up the Gallatin River to present-day Bozeman, Montana, and followed Sacajawea's directions to Bozeman Pass, leading to the Yellowstone River. Everyone planned to meet at the junction of the Yellowstone and Missouri Rivers.

…while Lewis goes to Great Falls

With the Louisiana Purchase in 1803, President Jefferson bought all the land that drained into the Missouri. Thus, knowing the Missouri River's northernmost tributary was important, Captain Lewis wanted to see where the Marias River's headwaters were. He and nine men took the Indian's overland route from Lolo Pass to Great Falls. Six men were left at Great Falls to make carts and help portage the canoes Sgt. Gass's detachment would bring down the Missouri. On July 11 Lewis took three men and headed north to find the headwaters of the Marias River.

Next episode, we will learn more about that deadly journey.

CAPTAIN MERIWETHER LEWIS
of the Lewis and Clark Expedition, accompanied by three of his men, explored this portion of the country upon their return trip from the coast. On July 26 1806, they met eight Piegans (Blackfeet), who Lewis mistakenly identified as Gros Ventres, and camped with them that night on Two Medicine Creek at a point northeast of here. Next morning the Indians, by attempting to steal the explorers' guns and horses, precipitated a fight in which two of the Indians were killed.
This was the only hostile encounter with Indians that the Expedition encountered in their entire trip from St. Louis to the Pacific and back. Lewis unwittingly dropped a bombshell on the Piegans with the news that their traditional enemies the Nez Perce, Shoshoni and Kootenai, were uniting in an American-inspired peace and would be getting guns and supplies from Yankee traders. This threatened the Blackfeet's 20 year domination of the Northern Plains made possible by Canadian guns.

CAMP DISAPPOINTMENT
The monument on the hill above was erected by the Great Northern Railway in 1925 to commemorate the farthest point north reached by the Lewis and Clark Expedition. 1804-06. Captain Meriwether Lewis. with three of his best men left the main party at the Missouri River and embarked on a side trip to explore the headwaters of the Marias River. He hoped to be able to report to President Jefferson that the headwaters arose north of the 49th parallel, thus extending the boundaries of the newly acquired Louisiana Purchase.
The party camped on the Cut Bank River July 22-25. 1806. in a "beautifull and extensive bottom." Deep in the territory of the dreaded Blackfoot the men were uneasy. Lewis wrote "game of every discription is extreemly wild which induces me to believe the indians are now, or have been lately, in this neighbourhood." Lewis could see from here that the river arose to the west rather than to the north, as he had hoped. Disheartened by this discovery by the cold rainy weather and by the shortage of game Lewis named this farthest point north Camp Disappointment. the actual site of which is four miles directly north of this monument.

Two contemporary Montana road signs. Note that the second of these indicates "Camp" Disappointment, not "Cape" Disappointment at the mouth of the Columbia. To most motorists and tourists the most visible and lasting impression of the Expedition today are these ubiquitous road signs and trail indicators. Most of the original routes and trails remain difficult to reach and explore.

EPISODE 25

Death on the Trail

The day Lewis and Clark had long feared had arrived. One Indian was dead and another either dead or seriously wounded. After 2-1/2 years of traveling through Indian country without any major problems, how could this have happened? President Jefferson had given Lewis written instructions to treat Indians "in the most friendly & conciliatory manner which their own conduct will admit." While there had been some tense moments as the Corps crossed paths with hostile Indians, they had been able to use diplomacy to resolve conflicts in each case. At least, until July 26, 1806.

Divide and conquer

On July 3, after crossing the Rocky Mountains, the Corps split into several parties to further explore the northern plains. Lewis and nine men went to Great Falls using an overland route the Nez Perce had told him about. He left six men there to construct carts to portage the canoes that Sgt. Ordway would be bringing down the Missouri.

Lewis took his three best men and headed north to determine if the headwaters of the Marias River lay above the 49th parallel; the United States owned all the land drained by the Missouri River.

Lewis was well aware of the danger in this mission, since it would require traveling across Blackfeet land. Lewis's fear was based on experiences of other Indian tribes that had been victims of the aggressive Blackfeet nation. Lewis wrote they were a *"vicious lawless and reather an abandoned set of wretches"* and he was determined *"to avoid an interview with them if possible."*

After traveling up the Marias River, only to find it did not go as far north as he hoped, Lewis decided to return to the Missouri River and rejoin the Expedition. On the morning of July 26, they left their camp near present-day Cut Bank, Montana, and proceeded down Two Medicine River. That afternoon, Lewis saw the thing he had feared most — a group of Indians coming towards them.

Strength in numbers

It appeared Lewis and his men were heavily outnumbered; the Indians had 30 horses, about half wearing saddles. Lewis wrote, *"this was a very unpleasant sight."* He unfurled his flag and rode towards the Indians. After both sides met, Lewis was relieved to find just eight young Indians herding horses captured in a raid, but he noticed two Indians had muskets obtained from French-Canadian fur traders. After giving his last peace medal to a chief, Lewis wrote, *"I was convinced that they would attempt*

... scene of the crime? ...

The purported site of this incident was discovered in 1964 by two Cut Bank Boy Scout leaders who used the directions and descriptions contained in Lewis's journal. Two of the 'three solitary trees' described by Lewis in his journal still stand, and the site has been marked and fenced by the local Boy Scout District and has been declared a historic site by the National Park Service. As part of the Bicentennial Commemoration in 2006, the Blackfeet Tribe organized a four-day symposium memorializing the fight. "The symposium will advance the Bicentennial's top priorities of expressing American Indians' perspectives about Lewis and Clark and examining our shared history from diverse, sometimes divergent, points of view," said a tribal spokesperson.

to rob us in which case... I should resist to the last extremity prefering death to that of being deprived of my papers instruments and gun." Lewis invited the Indians to spend the night together in order to prevent them from returning to their village for reinforcements.

Lewis told his men they needed to watch the Indians all night to prevent them from stealing their guns and horses. After smoking with the Indians until dark, Lewis took the first watch. When he woke Reuben Fields at midnight, the Indians all appeared to be asleep. His brother, Joseph, took the next watch. All went well until daybreak, when the Indians got up and crowded around the fire.

In the blink of an eye

According to Lewis, Joseph Fields *"carelessly laid his gun down behind him near where his brother was sleeping."* Before he knew it, the Indian wearing the peace medal took both of the Fields brothers' rifles. Worse, two other Indians had slipped up to where Lewis and George Drouillard were sleeping and stole their rifles. When Joseph Fields saw what was happening, he yelled out to his brother. Reuben Fields jumped up and chased the Indian with the two rifles for 150 feet when, according to Lewis's journal, *"he seized his gun, stabed the indian to the heart with his knife... the fellow ran about 15 steps and fell dead."*

Lewis awoke to hear Drouillard shouting, *"damn you let go my gun."* Drouillard recovered his rifle, but when Lewis realized his rifle was also gone, *"drew a pistol from my holster"* and ran after the Indian who had taken it. After Lewis warned the Indian he was going to shoot him, the Indian *"droped the gun and walked slowly off, I picked her up instantly."* All four rifles were recovered and no shots had been fired. But, one Indian lay dead.

Lewis's men wanted to kill the Indians, but Lewis refused, saying the Indians had not tried to harm them. But things soon changed when the Indians attempted to steal their horses. Lewis wrote, *"I pursued the man who had taken my gun who with another was driving off a part of the horses... being nearly out of breath I could pursue no further, I called to them... that I would shoot them if they did not give me my horse."*

Now what?

Lewis wrote, as he *"raised my gun, one of them jumped behind a rock and spoke to the other who turned arround and stoped at the distance of 30 steps from me and I shot him through the belly, he fell to his knees and on his wright elbow from which position he partly raised himself and fired at me, and turning himself about crawled in behind a rock which was a few feet from him. he overshot me, being bearheaded I felt the wind of his bullet very distinctly."* Most historians believe the Indian Lewis shot died, but he possibly survived.

... Lewis was concerned ...

"I drove up that same path on my visit to the area, trying to relive it. And that's out in the middle of nowhere, desolate, dry land. And I'm thinking, 'Okay, they're out there, and they see these Indians coming at them.' And I'm sure they felt like they were going to die. And there were only three of them, and eight or ten Indians coming. And I think that's probably the one time that Lewis feared being outnumbered or out-gunned by the Indians on the whole trip. Up 'til then, they'd had the cannon on the boat and other weapons that they could shoot and scare them off."

Lewis was concerned that the Indians who escaped would return, so the men rounded up the remaining horses, some of which belonged to the Indians. After throwing the Indians' bows and arrows onto the campfire, Lewis left the peace *"medal about the neck of the dead man that they might be informed who we were."* Then, they mounted their horses and rode 120 miles in 24 hours.

Safe at last

They arrived at the mouth of the Marias River just as Sergeant Gass and his party came floating down the Missouri. Lewis wrote, *"I was so soar from my ride yesterday that I could scarcely stand."* Now, if the Blackfeet managed to track them down, there were enough men and guns to repel an attack.

MORE TO THE STORY: A case of murder?

A BLACKFEET TRIBAL ELDER, G. G. Kipp, feels Lewis's story is false. However, no existing written record supports his belief. Indians did not have a written language; they relied on oral histories to pass down events to future generations.

According to Kipp (in a presentation to the Blackfeet Community College's Native American Scholars program, as reported in a 2003 Great Falls Tribune article), Lewis and his party ran into a group of young boys who were herding horses back to camp from a previous foray. "They stayed with them and gambled with them," Kipp said in 2003. "In the morning, they went to part company, and the Indians took what they had won. That was it," said Kipp, "that's when they were killed."

...or justifiable homicide?

A newspaper story dating back to 1919 offers another view. In 1895, George Bird Grinnell, one of the fathers of Glacier National Park, interviewed a 102-year old Blackfoot chief named Wolf Calf. He told Grinnell that when he was 13 years old, he and some other Indians met some white men in a friendly fashion. Their chief directed them to try to steal some things, according to Wolf Calf. He said they did so early the next morning, and the white men killed one of them with a big knife. When asked why the Indians didn't pursue Lewis to retaliate, Wolf Calf said they were frightened and ran away – just like Lewis and his men, but in the opposite direction.

Photo by Bob Wick, a BLM employee

Pompey's Pillar was designated as a National Monument in January 2001. Prior to its monument status, it was designated a National Historic Landmark in 1965. At the Pillar, there is evidence of Native Americans, early explorers, fur trappers, the U.S. Cavalry, railroad development and early homesteaders, many of whom left their history embedded in this sandstone monument. On July 25, 1806, Clark carved his signature and the date in the rock and recorded doing so in his journal. The historic signature remains today, and visitors can walk on a boardwalk to see it.

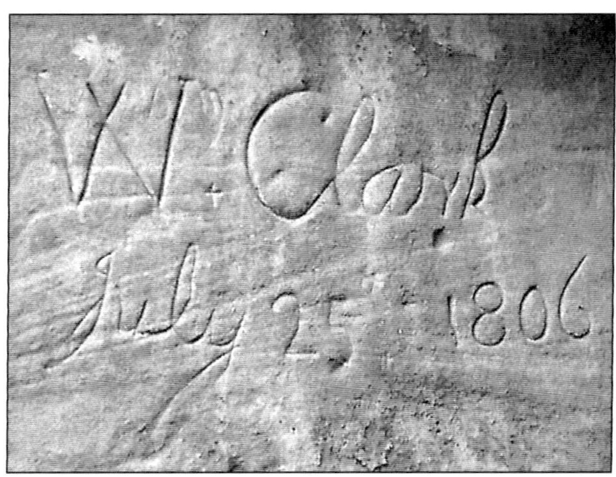

EPISODE 26

Graffiti Is Nothing New

ON JULY 25, 1806, CLARK SAW a "remarkable rock" near the bank of the Yellowstone River, 25-miles east of Billings, Montana. It was a large sandstone formation that stood 200 feet above the flat prairie. For centuries, Indians had painted pictographs and etched petroglyphs onto the sheer walls of the rock they called Iishiia Anaache ("Place Where the Mountain Lion Dwells"). The rock was a well-known landmark to the Plains Indians since it marked the location of a strategic natural crossing of the Yellowstone River. The rock would also become a significant landmark to early European explorers, fur trappers, immigrants and soldiers.

Clark climbed to the top to see what he could see, and then carved his name and the date in the rock. Today, that signature is the only physical evidence remaining to prove Lewis and Clark made the journey to the ocean and back. Clark named the outcropping "Pompy's Tower" after Sacajawea's 17-month old son Jean Baptiste Charbonneau (Clark had nicknamed him "Pomp."). The first editor of Lewis and Clark's journals, Nicholas Biddle, later changed the name to Pompey's Pillar.

Hundreds of individuals have carved their names on the rock over the last two centuries. While Clark's etching isn't as clear as it once was, it is still visible. In 1882, the Northern Pacific Railroad took steps to protect it with an iron screen; in 1953 a glass case was installed to protect it from the weather. The land was privately owned until 1991 when the Bureau of Land Management bought it. It was declared a national monument in 2001.

More than a Kick in the Pants

The previous episode covered the unfortunate death of one, possibly two, Blackfoot Indians. One of those Indians had shot at Captain Lewis, just missing his head. Lewis, Drouillard, and the two Fields brothers felt lucky to have escaped with their lives after that encounter. Up to then, the only other death during the journey had occurred two years earlier, on August 20, 1804, when Sgt. Charles Floyd died from what today is believed to have been a burst appendix. But, soon, death would be looking for Meriwether Lewis again.

While Lewis and his detachment explored the Marias River's headwaters, the two parties headed by Sgt. Gass and Ordway had met at Great Falls to portage the canoes and supplies cached

the previous year around the series of waterfalls. At the same time, Capt. Clark took a detachment, including Sacajawea, to explore the Yellowstone River. The plan was for everyone to meet at the mouth of the Yellowstone River. All this without GPS, let alone a road map!

Clark reached the rendezvous point where the Yellowstone and Missouri Rivers join near the Montana and North Dakota border on August 3rd and set up camp to wait for the others. The mosquitoes were horrible, so Clark left a note for Lewis to look for them downstream. Five days later, after escaping the mosquitoes, Clark was surprised to see Sgt. Pryor floating down the Missouri in a bullboat, made with buffalo hides stretched over a framework, sort of like an umbrella. Pryor and two others had left Clark on July 23rd to take the remaining horses to Fort Mandan in North Dakota, but two days later Indians stole the horses. The three men then walked east to the Yellowstone River and found Clark's note to Lewis. To Clark's dismay, Pryor had brought the note with him! However, on August 7th Lewis would find another note from Clark and would figure out what Clark had done.

Meanwhile, back in Montana...

After escaping with their lives on July 27th when at least one Indian was killed, Lewis and his three men needed to get to the mouth of the Marias River. He had told the Blackfoot Indians that there were more white men waiting for him there, so he needed to get there first in case the Indians decided to attack. They rode 120 miles in 24 hours, and when they arrived were happy to find the men led by Sgt. Gass and Ordway floating down the Missouri. While everyone felt security in numbers, no time was wasted; all their horses were turned loose, and everyone got into the canoes and headed downstream at seven miles per hour to meet Clark's group at the mouth of the Yellowstone.

Choose your hunting partner carefully...

After surviving for more than two years in the wilderness, the men of the Corps of Discovery had become excellent hunters. But, as Dick Cheney might acknowledge, things can go bad while hunting with friends. On August 11th, Lewis saw a herd of elk along the river. He and Pierre Cruzatte, a one-eyed Frenchman who didn't see all that well out of his good eye, landed to try to kill some. Each of them shot an elk, but Cruzatte's elk was only wounded and continued into the brush. After reloading, they each took separate routes in pursuit of the wounded elk.

... Shot in the butt ...

"They'd seen elk out there, and Lewis didn't typically go out but they needed the meat. So Lewis goes out with Cruzatte. And Cruzatte was the classic 'blind in one eye and nearsighted in the other,' and not a very good hunting partner. And the next thing you know, Lewis gets shot in the butt. A bad accident, but of course an accident. And the other guy would never admit it. All this proof and he denied it."

And, be careful of what you wear

Lewis wrote, "*I was in the act of firing on the Elk a second time when a ball struck my left thye; the stroke was very severe; I instantly supposed that Cruzatte had shot me by mistake for an Elk as I was dressed in brown leather and he cannot see very well; under this impression I called out to him damn you, you have shot me, and looked towards the place from whence the ball had come, seeing nothing I called Cruzatte several times as loud as I could but received no answer; I was now preswaded that it was an indian that had shot me as the report of the gun did not appear to be more than 40 paces from me and Cruzatte appeared to be out of hearing of me.*"

Who, me?

Lewis stumbled back to the river, calling out to Cruzatte along the way, warning him to retreat since there were Indians in the bushes. Upon reaching the river, Lewis told the men he "*was wounded but I hoped not mortally*" and then ordered the men to go back and try to save Cruzatte. Lewis attempted to lead the men back in the search for Cruzatte, but the pain was so bad he nearly passed out after a hundred paces. He ordered his men to continue the search while he limped back to the canoe. About 20 minutes later, the men returned with Cruzatte and reported they had seen no sign of Indians. Cruzatte said he had shot an elk after he and Lewis had split up, but denied shooting Lewis. Cruzatte "*absolutely denied*" hearing Lewis calling for help after being shot.

A little detective work

Lewis wrote, "*I do not believe that the fellow did it intentionally but after finding that he had shot me was anxious to conceal his knowledge of having done so... the ball had lodged in my breeches which I knew to be the ball of the short rifles as that he had, and there being no person out with me but him and no Indians that we could discover I have no doubt in my own mind of his having shot me.*" The .54 caliber ball was only used in the Model 1803 rifle, a gun that had not yet reached Indian hands.

Is there a doctor in the house?

Lewis wrote, "*I took off my cloaths and dressed my wounds myself as well as I could, introducing tents of patent lint into the ball holes, the wounds blead considerably but I was hapy to find that it had touched neither bone nor artery.*" The "tents" Lewis wrote about were rolls of lint used to keep the wound open and thus allow new tissue to grow from the inside out and promote drainage. Lewis's biggest danger was infection.

… made his last journal entry …

It's surprising that so little is made of Lewis's wounding and its effects. The fact that the Expedition's leader and chief chronicler suddenly goes silent for the last six weeks — especially given the problems he experienced later trying to write the trip's grand narrative — may have indicated the degree of his disabilities, both physical and psychological. In extreme pain, healing slowly, and debilitated, Lewis was seriously impaired, and it could be argued his tragic demise was foreordained from the time of the accident.

And we meet again

The next day, Lewis's party met a canoe coming up the Missouri. The two fur trappers told him they had passed Clark's group the day before. When the two parties finally rejoined later that day, Clark was quite alarmed to find Lewis lying in the bottom of the canoe, seriously wounded. Lewis believed he would be OK, saying it would take 20 to 30 days to heal. Clark wrote that he, *"examined the wound and found it a very bad flesh wound the ball had passed through the fleshey part of his left thy below the hip bone and cut the cheek of the right buttock for 3 inches in length and the depth of the ball."*

Lewis made his last journal entry of the Expedition on August 12th when he wrote, *"as wrighting in my present situation is extremely painfull to me I shall desist until I recover and leave to my frind Capt. C. the continuation of our journal."* Three weeks later, Clark reported Lewis was *"mending fast,"* and by September 4th he was able to walk comfortably.

The next episode will cover the Expedition's return to St. Louis.

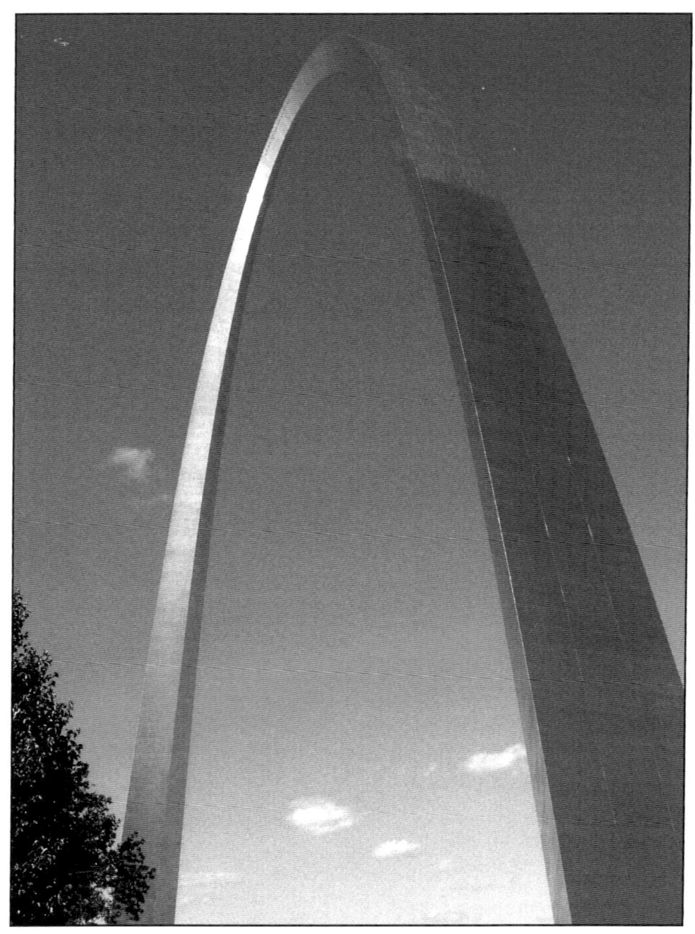

Lewis and Clark's Corps of Discovery returned to St. Louis on September 23, 1806, officially ending their 29-month exploration of the West. Located on the Missouri shore of the Mississippi River in St. Louis, the Gateway Arch is an elegant monument to the westward expansion that followed. There was a nationwide competition in 1948 to design a monument in St. Louis honoring western pioneers. Construction of the arch began in 1963, and it was finished in1965. The 630-foot tall stainless steel arch cost about $13 million to build and was opened to the public on July 24, 1967. Elevators carry people to the top and its viewing windows.

EPISODE 27

The Home Stretch

The last episode told about the accidental shooting of Captain Lewis by one of his own men on August 11, 1806. A day later, with Lewis lying on his stomach in the bottom of a canoe, his party caught up with Captain Clark in western North Dakota. It had been five weeks since the Corps of Discovery split up after crossing the Rocky Mountains, and somehow the entire party found their way to the meeting point at the junction of the Yellowstone and Missouri Rivers at the border of North Dakota and Montana, and was together once again and anxious to get to St. Louis.

Back at Fort Mandan

Two days later, they arrived at Fort Mandan where they had spent the winter of 1804. Clark wrote, "*Those people were extreamly pleased to See us.*" Sadly, their fort had burned while they were gone. However, Capt. Lewis had something he needed to do there. Before starting the journey in 1803, President Jefferson had told Lewis to bring some Indians with him when he returned to Washington, D.C. Lewis convinced Big White, a Mandan chief, to make the trip with his family and a French fur trapper who would serve as an interpreter.

Checking out Early

Private John Colter requested a discharge so he could join a couple of fur trappers who were heading up the Missouri. Colter had no desire to return to a "lonely" life in the civilized world. The captains agreed and, as Sgt. Ordway wrote in his journal, "*Settled with him and fitted him out with powder lead and a great number of articles which completed him for a trapping voyage of two years.*" Colter would soon discover the geysers and steam vents that today are part of Yellowstone National Park; however, when people heard about what he had seen, they thought he was crazy.

Goodbye to Sacajawea

At Fort Mandan, Clark wrote, "*we took our leave of T. Charbono, his Snake Indian wife and their son child, who had accompanied us on our rout to the pacific ocean in the capacity of interpreter and interpretess.*" Charbonneau was given a voucher for $500.33 for his services, but Sacajawea received nothing. Clark "*offered to take his little son, a butifull promising child who is about 19 months old*" to raise and provide the best education available. Clark wrote, "*They observed that in one year the boy would be Sufficiently old to leave his mother… if I would be so friendly as to raise the child in Such manner as I thought proper, to which I agreed.*" However,

Looking for "Captain Merry"

Even though Spain had officially given the Louisiana Territory to France in 1800, and France had sold the land to the United States in 1803, Spanish officials were not at all happy when they learned about the Lewis and Clark Expedition. Two months before the Corps set out from St. Louis in 1804, the Spanish military governor of Louisiana had given orders to arrest "Mr. Merry Weather Lewis, Captain of the Army of the United States."

Four different Spanish expeditions set out from Santa Fe in search of the Americans over a two-year period. The first, in August 1804, made it to the Platte River in central Nebraska, but Lewis and his party were already well north of there. A second effort in October 1805 ended almost as soon as it began when Indians attacked. In April 1806, a third effort failed due to mass desertions.

The final Spanish expedition set out in the summer of 1806, just as the Corps was heading down the Missouri from Fort Mandan. This time there were 105 Spanish soldiers, 400 New Mexico milita men, and 100 Indians. By September 1st, they had made it to a Pawnee village on the Republican River in south-central Nebraska. If they had continued on for another week, they most likely would have met the Corps of Discovery at the junction of the Missouri and Platte Rivers. However, the Pawnees objected to the Spanish expedition; rather than push the issue, the Spaniards turned around and went back to Santa Fe. Who knows how the Lewis and Clark story might have ended if the Pawnees had let the Spanish forces proceed.

it wasn't until 1811, when Charbonneau went to St. Louis to redeem his voucher, that he and Sacajawea would leave Pomp with Clark.

It's Downhill all the Way

St. Louis was 1,500 miles downriver from Fort Mandan. On August 20th, Clark wrote they "only" traveled 81 miles that day; in 1804, while rowing upstream, they were lucky to travel a tenth of that distance in a day. On August 29th, Clark reported seeing a herd of at least 20,000 buffalo. Meat was once again plentiful and, with wild fruit such as pawpaws found along the river, everyone had enough to eat.

On September 4th, the men stopped at the grave of Sgt. Floyd who had died of a burst appendix on the journey up the Missouri in 1804. They discovered the grave had been opened by Indians, so they refilled it.

The Bar is Open!

On September 6th they met another trading party and Captain Clark bought a gallon of whiskey, *"the first Spititous licquor which had been tasted by any of them Since the 4 of July 1805"* at Great Falls, Montana. Some of the men traded to get linen shirts to replace their buckskin clothing. A few days later, Lewis had healed enough to walk with ease and could even run a little.

Another group of traders told Lewis that Jefferson had sent out two more expeditions to explore the Louisiana Purchase: Zebulon Pike explored the Rockies in what is now Colorado, and the Freeman-Custis expedition went up the Arkansas and Red Rivers. They also learned that the Arikara chief who had gone to visit President Jefferson in 1805 had died in Washington, D.C.

Breaking News

The party passed several Indian villages and met dozens of trappers and traders heading upstream. They stopped to obtain news from the United States, in exchange for information about what was upstream. They learned that Thomas Jefferson had been re-elected president, that Aaron Burr had killed Alexander Hamilton in a duel in 1804, that war had been declared, waged, and won against Tripoli, and that relations with England and Spain were strained and war seemed possible. They also learned the Spanish army had been looking for them during the last two years, and that many people thought they had been captured. *"We had been long Since given up by the people of the U.S. and almost forgotton."* But Clark was told, *"the President of the U. States had yet hopes for us."*

Approaching civilization

On September 20th, the men let out a cheer when they saw cattle in a field – a sure sign they were approaching civilization. Clark wrote that the men "*Sprung upon their ores*" as they approached a village, and fired a salute that was answered by boats at the dock. "*Every person, both French and Americans, Seem to express great pleasure at our return, and acknowledged themselves much astonished in Seeing us return. They informed us that we were Supposed to have been long lost Since.*" A day later they arrived in St. Charles and again were greeted by people who were surprised to see them alive. The men saw women walking along the river, and with "*great dexterity*" they rowed to shore for a closer view of the first white women they had seen in more than two years.

Home at Last!

After traveling 8,000 miles in 28 months, they arrived back in St. Louis on September 23, 1806. A messenger from St. Charles had informed the thousand citizens of St. Louis that the Corps of Discovery was coming. John Ordway wrote the men, "*Fired three Rounds as we approached,*" and "*The people gathered on the Shore and Huzzared three cheers.*" After landing, Lewis immediately asked when the next mail dispatch was scheduled and was told it had already left. He sent a messenger to hold the mail until the next day so he could write a letter to President Jefferson.

Dear Tom...

Lewis spent most of the night writing. He opened his long letter by saying, "*It is with pleasure that I announce to you the safe arrival of myself and party at 12 OClk. today... In obedience to your orders we have penetrated the Continent of North America to the Pacific Ocean... and sufficiently explored the interior of the country to affirm with confidence that we have discovered the most practicable rout which dose exist across the continent by means of the navigable branches of the Misouri and Columbia Rivers.*" He went on to explain that there was no all-water route; Jefferson's vision of a Northwest Passage had been put to rest. It would take a full month for his letter to reach Jefferson.

The men had succeeded in their mission and the Expedition was over. There was still a lot of work to be done to study all the information and all the plant, animal, and geological samples they brought back. And, there would be a book to write.

THE

Legacy

... who had the strongest? ...

"We knew we had the weaker claim. The question was who had the strongest? And we're used to assuming that Britain and France and Russia, to a certain degree, were the ones that did all the expeditions. The truth is that Spain was here long before and they actually had maps of all this coast, but they didn't share them with anybody. They took it all back and locked it up."

EPISODE 28

The Expedition Returned ... Then What?

In 2002, David Plotz wrote an article about the Lewis and Clark Expedition titled "Stop Celebrating – They Don't Matter" (viewable on the Internet). While Plotz wrote that the Lewis & Clark Expedition was irrelevant and insignificant, most historians believe they opened the door to American settlement of the West. Without the Corps of Discovery, the U.S. would have had a weaker claim to the land that eventually became Washington and Oregon. It is even possible we might have ended up as part of Canada. However, Plotz makes some very good points in his article.

My wife and I have enjoyed a couple of vacations in Scotland. One of my favorite spots is the Isle of Lewis (no relation to Meriwether Lewis) and the Isle of Harris. Progress has bypassed these Outer Hebrides Islands to a large degree – only one town of any size, and no fast food restaurants. The people mostly fish and raise sheep; the wool is made into the famous Harris Tweed on treadle looms in private homes. Listening to the old women tell about how long it took to create the fabric using the old techniques made me realize how easy it is to take progress for granted.

While half the members of the Corps of Discovery were born before the United States became a country in 1776, most of those men would have been too young to remember America's War of Independence. Captain Lewis was born in 1774, Captain Clark in 1770, and Seargant Gass in 1771. All the men had seen the United States grow in its first 30 years, and many would live long enough to see even greater change, and I was intrigued to learn one member of the Lewis & Clark Expedition lived to be almost 100. Oh, what he saw in his lifetime!

A lot can happen in a century

Think about it: Someone born a hundred years ago would have witnessed the beginnings of flight that led to today's commercial airlines – and to the space program that put men on the moon just 66 years after the Wright brothers flew their first airplane at Kitty Hawk in 1903. They would have experienced the rapid development of the automobile and a network of highways that ties our country together. They watched silent, black and white movies develop into talkies and then into color. They experienced the transition from radio to television, they listened to music on Edison phonographs and saw the development of stereo phonographs, reel-to-reel tape recorders, 4-track and 8-track tapes, cassette tapes, CDs, and then digital music on

... the first American settlement ...

"I feel that the most important thing the expedition did was simply strengthen our territorial claim. Some people cite Astoria, but that's pretty fickle. John Jacob Astor's people come out in 1811 and build Astoria. A year later, the War of 1812 breaks out. And so the North West Company, the British Trading Company, goes to Astoria and tells the guy in charge, 'either you sell your fort to us — the war ship's coming around — or when it gets here, we're going to take it.' So they sold it to them. It became Fort George."

The Series 1901 United States $10 Note. Nicknamed the "Buffalo Bill," it was issued to stimulate interest in the Lewis and Clark Centennial Exposition held in Portland, Oregon, in 1905. The left portrait shows Meriwether Lewis, while the right portrait shows William Clark.

computers and iPods. They gave up their slide rules for hand-held calculators – and watched as computers and smart phones took over the world.

While many of the 33 people who went to the Pacific Ocean and back died early deaths, Patrick Gass was 99 when he died in 1870. He must have been amazed at how fast the West was settled. So, for this column, I thought it would be fun to list some of the important developments that took place during the lives of the members of the Corps of Discovery, after their return in 1806.

Running bare

Several men joined trapping parties to return to the western lands they had explored. The first man to die was Joseph Field, just a year after the Expedition ended. A year later, John Potts was killed by some Blackfeet Indians while John Colter, who discovered the geyser basins at Yellowstone, was stripped of all his clothing and managed to escape the Indians, running naked for five days before reaching Fort Raymond in Montana.

In 1809, the year James Madison became our fourth president, Captain Lewis and three others died; Lewis probably committed suicide (more on that in upcoming episodes). In 1810, George Drouillard was killed by Blackfeet Indians near Three Forks, Montana. One might wonder if this was a revenge killing, since he had been with Lewis when at least one Blackfeet Indian was killed there in 1806.

Astoria, the first American settlement on the Pacific coast, was founded in 1811. Two Corpsmen were in New Madrid, Missouri, when two of the most powerful earthquakes ever to strike North America (both magnitude ~7.5) occurred in December 1811 and February 1812. Several members of the Expedition participated in the War of 1812. Most historians think Sacajawea died in 1812, but some people believe she lived to be about 100, dying in 1884 (more on in an upcoming episode).

By 1817, when James Monroe became our fifth president, at least a dozen Corpsmen were dead. In 1825, when John Quincy Adams became our sixth president, the Hudson Bay Company established Fort Vancouver. Andrew Jackson became our seventh president in 1829 and Nathaniel Pryor died two years later, a year before the siege of the Alamo. At least 25 of the 33 men were dead when Captain Clark died in 1838.

Westward, Ho!

In 1840 there were just three states west of the Mississippi River (Louisiana, Missouri and Arkansas). A group of 100 emigrants headed west by wagon train in 1841; a thousand people made

The most common reminders of the Expedition's routes are familiar to western travelers.

the trip in 1843, followed by 2,000 in 1844 and 5,000 in 1845. By 1866, a half million people had left their homes in the east to travel to new homes in the west — a third of those came to Oregon and Washington. Towns were springing up all over the place as the flood of people arrived.

In 1844, Skamokawa and Oregon City were founded. St. Helens was founded in 1845 (originally called Plymouth), and Cathlamet was started in 1846. Peter Crawford filed a land claim in 1847 for what would become Kelso (it was not platted until 1884). The Oregon Territory was created in 1848. Monticello (located near the mouth of the Cowlitz River) was established in 1850, the same year California became a state. Rainier (originally called Eminence) was founded in 1851, and Woodland was settled a year later. The Washington Territory was created in 1853, and Oregon became a state in 1859.

Only three members of the Expedition were still alive when Abraham Lincoln was elected our sixteenth president in 1860. The Civil War began the following year and ended in 1865 when Robert E. Lee surrendered. A week later, Lincoln was assassinated; Alexander Willard had died a month earlier at age 86. Sacajawea's son, Pomp, died in 1866 and is buried in southeastern Oregon (his story will be told next episode).

And then there was just one

In 1868, Colonel George Custer made his last stand against the Cheyenne Indians. In 1869, the transcontinental railroad was completed at Promontory Point, Utah; by then, twenty states had been admitted to the union since the Corps returned to St. Louis in 1806. Patrick Gass died in 1870 at age 99, the same year Kalama was established. While he was the last member of the Expedition to die, he had married a 20-year old woman in 1831 (when he was 60) and had fathered seven children — some lived into the twentieth century. I've always wondered why nobody in his family wrote a book about their father's stories.

Now, we will wrap up by examining what happened to Sacajawea and her son Pomp. We will look at why nobody did anything with the maps that William Clark had worked so hard to create during the trip. And, we will learn more about what Captains Lewis and Clark did after they returned to St. Louis in 1806. You might think the journey is over, but is it, really?

"Lewis and Clark Reach the Shoshone Camp Led by Sacajawea"
by Charles M. Russell

EPISODE 29

What Happened to Sacajawea?

When the Lewis and Clark Expedition returned to the Mandan villages in 1806, Toussaint Charbonneau (Sacajawea's husband) was given a voucher for $500.33 for his services, but Sacajawea received nothing. In a letter to Charbonneau, Clark wrote, "Your woman who accompanied you that long dangerous and fatiguing rout to the Pacific Ocean and back diserved a greater reward for her attention and services on the rout than we had the power to give her at the Mandans."

Clark offered to take Pomp back to St. Louis where he would educate "and raise him as my own child." Sacajawea and Charbonneau agreed to let Clark raise their 18-month old son, but felt it was too soon to do so. In a letter, Clark wrote, "Charbono, if you wish to live with the white people, and will come to me, I will give you a piece of land and furnish you with horses, cows, & hogs."

Three years later, Charbonneau, Sacajawea, and Pomp traveled to St. Louis to cash his voucher. Charbonneau was given 320 acres of land, but after a year he decided he was not meant to be a farmer and sold the land back to Clark for $100. He left 5-year old Pomp in the care of Clark in 1811 and took Sacajawea back up the Missouri River. However, since Clark had married two years earlier, he did not actually raise Pomp as his "own child" as he had promised. Instead, he put Pomp in a boarding house and paid for his schooling.

Will the "real" Sacajawea please stand up?

On December 20, 1812, John Luttig, the clerk at Fort Manuel, a trading post on the upper Missouri in present-day South Dakota, included a terse obituary in his daily log: "This evening the wife of Charbonneau, a Snake squaw, died of a putrid fever. She was a good and the best woman in the Fort. Aged about 25 years. She left a fine infant girl." Even though her actual name does not appear in the record, many people believe it was Sacajawea who had died about four months after giving birth to a daughter.

Was this really Sacajawea? Probably. Sacajawea would have been about 24 years old in 1812. Toussaint Charbonneau had gone to Fort Manuel in 1811 shortly after leaving his son, 5-year old Pomp (Jean Baptiste), with Captain Clark in St. Louis. Believing Charbonneau to be dead, Luttig took Charbonneau's daughter to St. Louis in 1813, where the Orphan's Court made Luttig legal guardian of two Charbonneau children (one-year old "Lisette" and ten-year- old "Tousant"). Who was this "Tousant?" Most people believe this was an error, and the records actually refer to seven-year old Pomp ("Jean Baptiste"). Why would a

judge have allowed Luttig to become legal guardian for Pomp? Pomp had been under Captain Clark's care for two years, attending a private school, but Clark was away on business at the time. And why do the records show the boy was ten years old when Pomp was only seven? In any case, Luttig's name was later crossed out in the court records and the name of William Clark substituted.

So, who was the ten-year-old "Tousant Charbonneau" shown on the legal papers? Some people believe Charbonneau's other Shoshone wife (Otter Woman) gave birth to a son in 1803, three years before Pomp was born. Thus, it is uncertain which Shoshone wife Luttig's obituary pertains to. Charbonneau may have abandoned Sacajawea after returning to the Mandan villages from their 1811 visit to St. Louis when Pomp was left with Clark. Perhaps he took Otter Woman and her son to Fort Manuel.

William Clark's cashbook for 1825-1828 showed the status of all the Expedition members and states "*Se car ja we au Dead.*" However, since that same cashbook erroneously lists Sergeant Patrick Gass as being dead (he lived to be 99-years old, dying in 1870), some people think Clark could have been wrong in listing Sacajawea as being dead.

In 1884, on the Wind River Indian Reservation in present-day Wyoming, a Shoshone woman named Porivo, said to be about 100 years old, was laid to rest. Sacajawea would have been about 96 years old in 1884. The burial records said Porivo was "Bazil's mother (Shoshone)." When the Lewis and Clark expedition reunited Sacajawea with her Shoshone Indian tribe at Three Forks in 1805, she learned most of her family was dead, so she immediately adopted the young son of her dead sister. Could this be "Bazil"?

Bazil was living with his mother when she died. For years, this woman had told people she had been with Lewis and Clark on the expedition to the Pacific Ocean and that her son Baptiste was a little papoose whom she carried on her back from the Mandan villages across the shining mountains to the great lake. It seems odd an Indian woman living in Wyoming could have known so much about the woman who accompanied the Corps of Discovery 80 years earlier. One has to wonder if she might indeed have been the real Sacajawea!

Statues of Sacajawea with her 9-month old son "Pomp" on her back and Captain Lewis's Newfoundland dog, Seaman, were created by Heather Soderberg in 2011, located at Cascade Lock's Marine Park.

Pomp's Circumstances

By Gary Meyers

MENTION "SACAJAWEA," and most folks associate the name either with the Shoshone Indian woman who accompanied the Lewis and Clark Expedition, or the U.S. dollar first minted in 2000. Longview, Washington residents will also associate the name with their beautiful lake in the center of town.

While Sacajawea is known to generations of students and history buffs, oddly, few remember her son, Jean Baptiste Charbonneau. His remarkable beginning with the Corps of Discovery, combined with his later experiences as a trader, guide, interpreter, miner, adventurer and world traveler remain an extraordinary story, even today.

Jean Baptiste was born at Fort Mandan (North Dakota) on February 11, 1805. His father was a French-Canadian fur trader, Toussaint Charbonneau, who had joined the expedition as guide and interpreter.

Within months of birth, Jean Baptiste began his odyssey, bundled and strapped to his mother's back. Accounts indicate that he was a happy and healthy baby, well protected and treated as very special by the expedition members. Captain Clark took an immediate liking to the toddler and nicknamed him "Pomp" or "Pompy" (spellings differ).

By the time the expedition eventually reached the Pacific Ocean and returned to North Dakota, Pomp was nearly two years old and had ridden over 5,000 miles, enduring along the way hardships unimaginable by today's standards.

Clark's affection for the boy was, perhaps, best measured when the expedition reached a prominent sandstone butte on the Yellowstone River that Clark named Pompy's Tower (now called Pompey's Pillar). Pompey's Pillar remains today the only existing evidence of the Corps of Discovery along the trail; Captain Clark carved his name and date — Jul 25, 1806 — into the body of the rock.

Following the Corps of Discovery, Captain Clark provided Pomp with what has been described as, "the best education that money could buy." At age 16, with his education completed, Pomp struck out on his own as a fur trader. He made a chance acquaintance that would have a profound effect on his future.

Prince Paul Wilhelm was a German noble who was visiting the United States on a nature study. He and Pomp immediately became friends, and Pomp accepted Prince Wilhelm's invitation to accompany him back to Germany.

As a guest of the prince, Pomp traveled throughout Europe and North Africa, meeting royalty, enjoying the perks and privileges of the aristocratic class and also finding the time to learn several languages. After six years, however, he had tired of the rarified life of royalty and returned to his roots on the Great Plains.

For the next 15 years, Pomp roamed the west, living off the land as a "mountain man." He hunted. He trapped. He served as a guide for groups moving west. He did a short stint in the Army leading a Mormon battalion from Sante Fe to San Diego. He served briefly as the Alcalde (mayoral or magistrate status) of Mission San Luis Rey in Southern California.

When gold was discovered at Sutter's Fort, California, in 1849, the fever swept up Pomp and he headed north to seek his fortune. The fortune never materialized and little is known of Pomp's activities for several years thereafter.

In 1861, he re-surfaced as a clerk in the Orleans Hotel in Auburn, California. When news of another gold strike in Montana reached Auburn, Pomp grabbed his bags and headed toward the El Dorado that had eluded him earlier.

Sadly, his hope was not fulfilled. Pomp contracted pneumonia and died at Inskip Station, near Danner in Southeast Oregon on May 16, 1866, at age 61. He was buried there.

Note about the author: As a child, Gary Meyers lived in Ponca, Nebraska, where his curiosity about Lewis and Clark was piqued by three nearby sites mentioned in the journals. He later lived in Longview, Washington, and years later, upon reading Michael Perry's column, "Dispatch from the Discovery Trail,"wrote this piece on Pomp for Columbia River Reader. Meyers's contribution has become a regular component of the series.

Meriwether Lewis (1774–1809), by Charles Willson Peale

EPISODE 30

The End of the Journey for Meriwether Lewis

After the triumphant return of the Corps of Discovery, Meriwether Lewis's life spiraled downward until, on October 11, 1809, the 35-year old lay dead in a pool of blood. What happened? How could this be?

A new job and life's a mess

Upon their return to St. Louis in 1806, Lewis and Clark, along with Big White, a Mandan Indian chief, headed east to meet with Thomas Jefferson. In 1807, President Jefferson made Captain Lewis governor of the Upper Louisiana Territory and gave him 1,400 acres of land. It took a year for Lewis to report to his new position in St. Louis, and he soon realized he was not suited for the job. Piles of paperwork relating to land claims, quarrels and feuds among Indian trading companies, and partisan politics made Lewis wish he had never accepted the appointment.

His personal life had begun to fall apart, as well. While Lewis courted several women, none would agree to marry him. He drank too much and was taking opium to help him sleep. Both William Clark and President Jefferson were concerned about the lack of progress on the three-volume set of books Lewis had promised to write about the Corps of Discovery. After his initial efforts in 1806 to obtain help in publishing the proposed book, Lewis apparently never wrote a single page of the manuscript.

After losing money in land speculation, he grew more depressed as debts mounted up. Worst of all, Lewis felt his honor had been tarnished when he was formally rebuked in July 1809 for unauthorized expenditures, and the government refused to pay some of his vouchers. A month later, Lewis decided he had to go to Washington to plead his case in person. Part of his reason for going may have been to deliver the original Lewis and Clark expedition journals to a publisher in Philadelphia.

When Lewis met with Clark in St. Louis to explain his problems, he turned over deeds to his land to Clark to be used to pay his debts. Clark could see Lewis was in poor health, both physically and mentally. He tried to talk him out of the trip, but Lewis insisted on going. On September 4, Lewis and John Pernier, his free mulatto servant, along with Lewis's Newfoundland dog named Seaman, boarded a keel boat going from St. Louis to New Orleans.

...Lewis was shot and died...

The controversy over Lewis's death has continued to follow the Expedition and preoccupy subsequent historians. One certain, and tragic, fact is that Lewis suffered severely from depression and led an unhappy few years following his great feat of exploration. "At the end of his life he was a horrible drunk, terribly depressed, who could never even finish his journals," says Paul Douglas Newman, a professor of history who teaches "Lewis and Clark and The Early American Republic" at the University of Pittsburgh. In an article in Smithsonian Magazine, Newman concludes that, "He came back and he just could not readjust. On the mission it was 'how do we stay alive and collect information?' Then suddenly you're heroes. There's a certain amount of stress to reentering the world. It was like coming back from the moon."

Journey to the Big Easy: not so easy!

Lewis became ill during the trip, possibly from malaria he contracted in 1803. His journal contained several references to "bilious fever" and "pills of opium and tartar." Lewis wrote a will on September 11th designating his mother as his sole beneficiary. The boat arrived at Fort Pickering (near present-day Memphis) on September 15. Gilbert Russell, the Fort's commander, later wrote that Lewis had been drinking heavily and was in "a state of mental derangement." The keelboat's crew told him Lewis had "made two attempts to Kill himself, in one of which he had nearly succeeded." Lewis was put on a 24-hour suicide watch "until he recovered" a week later.

Detour to Nashville

Lewis originally planned to take a ship from New Orleans to reach Washington, D.C., but the presence of British war ships in the Gulf of Mexico worried him. In a letter to President Madison, he wrote, "my fear of the original papers relative to my voyage to the Pacific ocean falling into the hands of the British has induced me to change my rout and proceed by land through the state of Tennisee to the City of washington."

The Natchez Trace was a 450-mile long trail from Natchez, Mississippi, to Nashville, Tennessee. James Neelly, an Indian agent, accompanied Lewis since robberies were common along the path. They left Fort Pickering with their two servants on September 29. During the night of October 10, two packhorses wandered off (one carried a trunk containing Lewis's Corps of Discovery journals). Major Neelly stayed behind to look for the horses while Lewis, who was very sick, rode ahead to a tavern, or inn, called Grinder's Stand (the two servants followed behind him). That night, Lewis was shot and died. No completely satisfactory explanation for his death has ever been found.

He said...

A week later, on October 18, Neelly wrote a letter to Jefferson saying that Robert Grinder had not been home when Lewis arrived, and that Mrs. Grinder, "discovering the governor to be deranged, gave him up the house & slept herself in one near it." Neelly went on to say, "His servant and mine slept in the stable loft some distance from the other houses. The woman reports that three o'Clock she heard two pistols fire off in the Governors room; the servants being awakened by her, came in but too late to save him. He had shot himself in the head with one pistol & a little below the Breast with the other - when his servant came in he says; 'I have done the business my good Servant, give me water.' He gave him some, he survived but a short time." Neelly said he didn't arrive until "some time after" Lewis had died from the two .69 caliper (5/8" diameter) pistol balls. Neelly had Lewis' two trunks forwarded to Washington, and told Jefferson

two more trunks had been left at Fort Pickering. But Neelly stole Lewis' horse, his silver watch, his rifle and both pistols. The money Lewis was carrying disappeared, too.

She said…

Eighteen months later, in May 1811, Mrs. Grinder told Alexander Wilson a story containing more details than found in Neelly's 1809 letter. "In the same room where he expired," Wilson wrote, "I took down from Mrs. Grinder the particulars of that melancholy event." She said Lewis "came there about sunset, alone, and inquired if he could stay for the night." When asked if he was traveling alone, he said two servants would arrive soon.

When Mrs. Grinder called Lewis to supper, he only ate a little before jumping up, "speaking to himself in a violent manner" with his face flushed, ranting about his enemies in Washington. Lewis suddenly calmed down, lit his pipe and remarked in a kind voice, "Madam this is a very pleasant evening."

Even though Mrs. Grinder had prepared a bed for Lewis, he told her he wanted to sleep on the floor and had his servant bring his bear and buffalo skins. Mrs. Grinder went to the kitchen by the main cabin to be with her four young children and a 13-year old slave girl. Unable to sleep, Mrs. Grinder heard Lewis walking back and forth and talking to himself "like a lawyer." Around 3am she heard a pistol shot and something falling on the floor, followed by "O Lord!" Then she heard a second pistol shot.

In the light of the moon?

A few minutes later Lewis was at her door, calling out: "O madam! Give me some water, and heal my wounds." Through cracks between the logs, Mrs. Grinder said she saw "Lewis stagger back and fall against a stump that stands between the kitchen and the room. He crawled for some distance, raised himself by the side of a tree where he sat for a minute" before crawling back to his room. She said Lewis later returned to her door seeking water.

How she saw all this is a mystery, since there had been a new moon just the night before. And with the waxing crescent moon setting at 6:21 pm the night Lewis died, the sky would have been pitch black!

Wilson wrote that after Mrs. Grinder "permitted him to remain for two hours in this most deplorable situation, she sent two of her children to the barn, her husband not being home, to bring the servants." She said they found Lewis lying on the bed in his cabin, still conscious. Lewis "uncovered his side and showed them where the bullet had entered; a piece of his forehead was blown off… He begged they would take his rifle and blow out his brains," in return for which "he would give them all the

MAREKULIASZ/SHUTTERSTOCK.COM

Meriwether Lewis monument and grave, on Natchez Trace Parkway, Tennessee. Controversy over Lewis's death has both his descendants and many scholars lobbying to exhume his body.

money he had in his trunk." He told them, "I am no coward, but I am so strong, so hard to die." He finally died around 7 am, "just as the sun rose above the trees." After Lewis was buried on the Grinder's property, his dog Seaman kept a vigil at the grave, refusing to eat, and soon died with grief.

Digging for the truth

Lewis's grave was opened in 1848 prior to Tennessee's construction of a 20-foot tall stone monument. A doctor examined Lewis's remains to verify they built it in the right place and, without any explanation, the committee wrote: "The impression has long prevailed that under the influence of disease of body and mind Governor Lewis perished by his own hands. It seems to be more probable that he died by the hands of an assassin." That was the first official mention of murder – and was the beginning of the many conspiracy theories that continue to this day!

Alternative facts?

In 1838, almost 30-years after Lewis died, an Arkansas schoolteacher visited Lewis's grave. He was able to locate and interview Priscilla Grinder in her home 25 miles north of the old tavern (it had burned to the ground). Mrs. Grinder, then a 68-year old widow, had revised her story. She said three men had arrived after Lewis and the two servants. They left when Lewis drew a pair of pistols and challenged them to a duel. Mrs. Grinder said she heard three shots that night and saw Lewis crawling across the road on his hands and knees. She was surprised to see the servants coming from the stables, because she thought they had shared the house with Lewis. She noticed Lewis's servant was wearing the clothing Lewis had arrived in. After searching for Lewis, the servants found him across the road, badly wounded and wearing old tattered clothes. They brought him back to the cabin where he soon died.

Whether these discrepancies were due to a blurred memory on the part of Mrs. Grinder or lies she had previously told, no one knows. However, Robert Smith, a post rider carrying mail along the Natchez Trace on the morning of October 11, 1809, reportedly came upon Lewis lying against a tree outside Grinder's Stand with a bullet wound in his head. These and other conflicting stories have fueled murder conspiracy theories for 180 years.

History repeats itself

After Lewis's death, his servant, John Pernier, traveled from Grinder's Stand to Virginia. Pernier had worked for President Jefferson from 1804 to 1807 before he became Lewis's servant.

What happened to Seaman

Not much is known about the Newfoundland dog Capt. Lewis bought for $20 in 1803. He was mentioned in the journals occasionally, and when some Indians stole him in 1806 on the return trip up the Columbia, Lewis was prepared to kill the Indians responsible if his dog wasn't returned. The last official reference to Seaman was on July 15, 1806, when Lewis wrote the *"musquetoes continue to infest us in such manner that we can scarcely exist. for my own part I am confined by them to my bier* [a raised bed] *at least 3/4 of the time. My dog even howls with the torture he experiences from them."*

No official record exists about Seaman's fate after Capt. Lewis died. However, there are intriguing clues. In 1814, Rev. Timothy Alden published a book that described an interesting dog collar he had found in an Alexandria, Virginia, museum that was inscribed, "The greatest traveler of my species. My name is SEAMAN, the dog of captain Meriwether Lewis, whom I accompanied to the Pacific ocean through the interior of the continent of North America."

Alden added a note in his book saying, "After the melancholy exit of gov. Lewis, his dog would not depart for a moment from his lifeless remains... he refused to take every kind of food, which was offered him, and actually pined away and died with grief upon his master's gave."

The museum was probably part of the Masonic Lodge in the Alexandria-Washington D.C. area that was established in 1812, the year Capt. Clark received a letter from a Lodge official thanking him for the "truly valuable Present made by you to our infant museum." Unfortunately, Seaman's collar doesn't exist today – a fire in 1871 destroyed many artifacts in the museum.

Pernier met with Jefferson on November 26, 1809, and told him Lewis had committed suicide. Jefferson accepted Pernier's judgment and later wrote Lewis "had from early youth suffered from hypochondriac affections... inherited by him from his father." Pernier also visited Lewis's family seeking $240 Lewis owed him for back wages. Lewis's mother refused to accept the story of suicide. Then, seven months after Lewis's death, the servant was dead. Pernier was described as "wretchedly poor and destitute" when he killed himself with an overdose of laudanum (tincture of opium) on April 29, 1810.

While it seems almost certain Lewis killed himself, some people feel he might have been the victim of a random murder, since he was a distinguished traveler with money and goods. Maybe the two servants killed Lewis for his money? Or, maybe Neelly was part of a political conspiracy that wanted him dead. Local legend holds that, a year after Lewis's death, Robert Grinder was brought before a grand jury on a warrant for Lewis's murder, but no records exist. So, yes, murder is a possibility. But if Lewis was shot by someone else, why didn't he tell Mrs. Grinder or John Pernier or Major Neelly's servant before he died? The debate will likely continue forever.

Next episode we will examine what Captain Clark did after he returned.

William Clark (1770 –1838), by Charles Willson Peale

EPISODE 31

Clark's Life...Afterwards

Meriwether Lewis and William Clark had been co-leaders of the Corps of Discovery. Both men are usually referred to as Captains, but in fact only Lewis held that rank. After Lewis invited Clark to join the Expedition as co-commander in 1803, the Army refused to promote Clark so he was officially only a Lieutenant during the journey. In 2001, President Bill Clinton signed a posthumous Captain's commission for William Clark.

About the time Lewis asked Clark to join the Expedition in 1803, Clark visited Congressman George Hancock in Virginia. Clark, who was 33 years old, was quite taken by two girls he saw riding horses on the estate. One girl, Judith "Julia" Hancock, was just 12, while the other girl (her cousin) was 14.

Some people think Clark asked permission to marry Julia during the visit, but that seems unlikely. While Clark expressed an interest in Julia, it appears Colonel Hancock refused to let Clark court Julia at that time. He may have acknowledged Clark's interest by telling Clark that if he could establish himself financially he would look favorably on his request. Perhaps one of Clark's incentives for joining Lewis on the Expedition was for the opportunity to secure fame and fortune so that he might win Julia for his wife.

Clark was clearly thinking about Julia in May 1805 when he named a river for her in Montana. While Clark made no mention about it in his journal, Lewis wrote, "*Cap C who assended this R. much higher than I did has ~~thought proper to~~ call it Judieths River.*" Lewis's writing and then crossing out the words "thought proper to" suggests he initially had doubts about the propriety of naming the river after Clark's future wife, but Lewis soon followed suit by naming the Marias River after his cousin.

Upon returning from the Pacific Ocean, Lewis and Clark traveled to Washington, D.C., to see President Jefferson. Clark went to Virginia to visit Julia Hancock in January 1807. Did he ask permission to marry her at that time? Nobody knows, but he wrote to his brother on January 22 indicating he would soon be married. He began a serious courtship and, by March 1807, Clark wrote to Lewis saying he was engaged. A year later, in January 1808, 37-year old Clark married 16-year old Julia. They had five children before she died 12 years later.

St. Louis became their home, and their first son (Meriwether Lewis Clark) was born in January 1809. Earlier, in August 1806, when the Corps returned to Fort Mandan in North Dakota,

Nicholas Biddle (1786 –1844)
by William Inman

The Curious Mr. Biddle

Nicholas Biddle has survived in history as a financier and banker who served a variety of presidents and ultimately ended up fighting with one — Andrew Jackson — over the banking system in the still fledgling United States. A man of varying tastes and talents, Biddle was a contributor to and later editor of Port Folio, the first U.S. literary journal. He served as secretary to James Monroe, while Monroe was President Jefferson's minister to England (1806–07). Apparently aware that the Lewis and Clark narrative was languishing, Biddle wrote "History of the Expedition of Captains Lewis and Clark" (1814) based on the explorers' notes provided to him by Clark. Due to pressures from his career in public service, he consigned the completion of the book to an assistant, Paul Allen, who ended up appearing as chief author and copyright holder. Biddle refused any financial reward for his efforts, insisting what there was should go to Clark. Today the "Biddle Book" remains probably the best — and very rare in the original — summary record of the Lewis and Clark Expedition.

Clark had offered to take Pomp, Sacajawea and Toussaint Charbonneau's one-and-a-half-year-old boy, to St. Louis to raise him as his own son. They agreed, but wanted to wait a year. By the time they brought Pomp to St. Louis in 1810, Clark was married and had his own son with another on the way, so rather than adopting 6-year old Pomp, he placed him in a private boarding school.

After Meriwether Lewis' apparent suicide in 1809, Clark took over the task of getting a book published about the Corps of Discovery. Even though that project had been given to Lewis, he had not written a single line of text in the three years following their journey.

In 1810, Clark arranged for George Shannon, one of the members of the Corps, to go to Philadelphia to help Nicholas Biddle, a lawyer, prepare the narrative of the Expedition. Shannon helped fill in missing details and helped Biddle bring everything together. Clark assisted by answering questions Biddle raised, and thus the book contained additional information not found in the daily journals.

By the time Biddle finished the book in 1813, his legal business was consuming all his time, so he hired Paul Allen to finish the project. Incredibly, when the two-volume book was published in 1814, there was no mention of Biddle anywhere. Instead, the title page proclaimed the book was "Prepared for the press by Paul Allen, Esquire." Perhaps Biddle wanted complete anonymity; it is inconceivable that Allen would have taken credit for the book unless Biddle wanted it that way.

Biddle had been promised half of all the profits from the 2,000 books produced, but he refused any payment – not even the $500 he had given Allen out of his own pocket. Biddle wanted Clark to receive all the profits, but it appears all Clark received was the copyright and the right to publish a second edition. Amazingly, two years after the book was published, Clark still had been unable to obtain a copy for himself! The book did not sell very well since it had been eight years since the Expedition was completed. As you might expect, original copies are very rare today and command extraordinary prices (a near perfect copy sold for $35,000 in 1967). Reprints of the book are available at the Fort Clatsop bookstore, and are highly recommended since it provides a fuller story than the actual journals.

After the Corps of Discovery returned to St. Louis in 1806, Clark's slave, York, asked for his freedom. York was about the same age as Clark, and had been his life-long slave companion. York had faithfully performed his share of the work required

This $1 gold coin was produced for the Lewis & Clark Centennial Exposition held in Portland, Oregon, in 1905. There were 10,025 coins produced with 1904 dates and 10,041 coins produced with 1905 dates. Meriwether Lewis is represented on the front and William Clark on the back. The proceeds from the sale of these coins financed the bronze memorial of Sacajawea erected in Portland's Washington Park, pictured on page 66.

during the Expedition, and Indians had been impressed with his black skin and great strength. His presence undoubtedly enhanced the prestige of the white strangers as the Corps visited isolated Indian tribes. York believed he had earned his freedom, but Clark disagreed.

So, once the Corps disbanded, York returned to his old life as a slave. He asked Clark to sell him to someone in Louisville so he could be closer to his wife, but Clark refused. York was very unhappy and from that point on Clark treated him harshly. About 10 years later, Clark finally granted York his freedom and set him up with a freight-hauling business in Kentucky. Rumors indicated that York failed in that business and died of cholera by 1832.

In 1820, Julia became ill and went to her father's estate in Virginia, where she died. A year later, their daughter died. In November 1821, Clark had recovered from his grief and married Harriet Radford, Julia's cousin (this was the 14-year old girl Clark had seen riding a horse with Julia in 1803). Harriet had three children from an earlier marriage, and had two more after marrying Clark.

Clark was appointed chief Indian agent and brigadier general of the militia for the Louisiana Territory in 1807. He participated in the War of 1812, and was appointed governor of the Missouri Territory in 1813. Surprisingly, Clark was defeated in the election for governor of the state of Missouri in 1820. Clark served as superintendent of Indian affairs from 1822 to 1838. His second wife died in 1831; Clark was 68 when he died in 1838. He had outlived two wives and three of his seven children. William Clark will long be remembered as one of America's great heroes.

The Verendrye marker is a thin lead plate, 8.5 by 6.5 inches and about 1/8-inch thick. The inscription on the front is in Latin and reads, "In the twenty-sixth year of the reign of Louis XV, the most illustrious Lord, the Lord Marquis of Beauharnois being Viceroy, 1741, Pierre Gaultier De La Verendrye placed this." That inscription is actually incorrect; Pierre Gualtier de la Verendrye did not bury the tablet in 1741 as written, but it was the only plate his two sons had. On the back side, a message in French was scratched to correct the errors: "Placed by the Chevalier de la Verendrye - Louis, Joseph, La Londette and Miotte the 30th of March 1743."

EPISODE 32

Who Arrived First?

While many people still believe Lewis and Clark were the first white men to explore the Great Plains, others wonder how the land included in the 1803 Louisiana Purchase initially came to be owned by France and Spain.

In 1738, Pierre Verendrye, a French fur trader living near present-day Winnipeg, Canada, visited a Mandan village near present-day Bismarck, North Dakota (about 60 miles south of where the Lewis and Clark Expedition spent their winter in 1804-1805). Mandan, Cheyenne, and Crow Indians told Verendrye about Spanish trading ships along the Pacific coast, fueling his desire to find a route to the Pacific Ocean.

In April of 1742, two of his sons, and at least two employees, set out from the Mandan village on an exploration that they hoped might end up at the "Western Sea." The Verendyne group was warned of the fierce Snake (Shoshone) Indians, so they made a long detour to avoid a potential conflict. Rather than following the Missouri River, they traveled southwest and west until, on January 1, 1743, they saw snow-capped mountains to the west which they reached eight days later (probably the Big Horn Mountains near present-day Sheridan, Wyoming).

Their Indian guides refused to go any further, so the group was forced to return without seeing what lay beyond the mountains. In March 1743, on their return trip, the Verendrye brothers buried an inscribed lead tablet on a bluff near present-day Pierre, South Dakota, claiming the land for France. The plate, discovered by accident in 1913 by school children, now resides in the South Dakota Cultural Heritage Center at Pierre.

Upon his return to Manitoba, Louis Verendrye wrote they had "added considerably to the geographical knowledge of the period; ensured for the Canadians and French the friendship and loyalty of... Indian tribes until then unknown... (and demonstrated) that the route to the western sea was not to be sought to the southwest, but to the northwest..."

However, members of the Verendrye expedition were not the first Europeans to explore the interior of North America. 200 years earlier, Spain's Francisco Vasquez de Coronado had led a large expedition from Mexico to near present-day Salina, Kansas, and was the first white man to see the Grand Canyon and the Colorado River. Coronado's journey took place 80 years before the Mayflower's Pilgrims landed near Plymouth Rock in 1620.

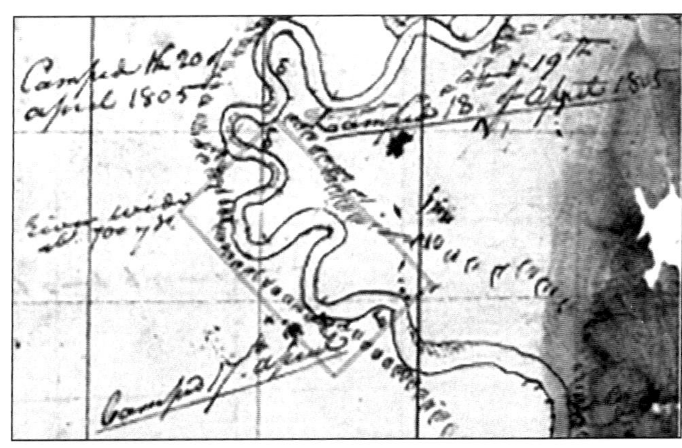

Below: A map from Martin Plamondon's "Lewis and Clark Trail Maps, Volume II." The box in Clark's map, at right, corresponds to the map below. Plamondon used the information in Clark's daily journals to determine identifiable starting and ending points that could be located on modern USGS topographic maps (typically, stream mouths, ox-bow bends, prominent buttes, etc.). Plamondon then attempted to plot Clark's traverse readings on the map. Clark's distances were consistently too long, and his bearings did not take magnetic declination into account (and often did not come close to fitting the lay of the land). Still, Clark's maps were remarkable considering the conditions under which they were made.

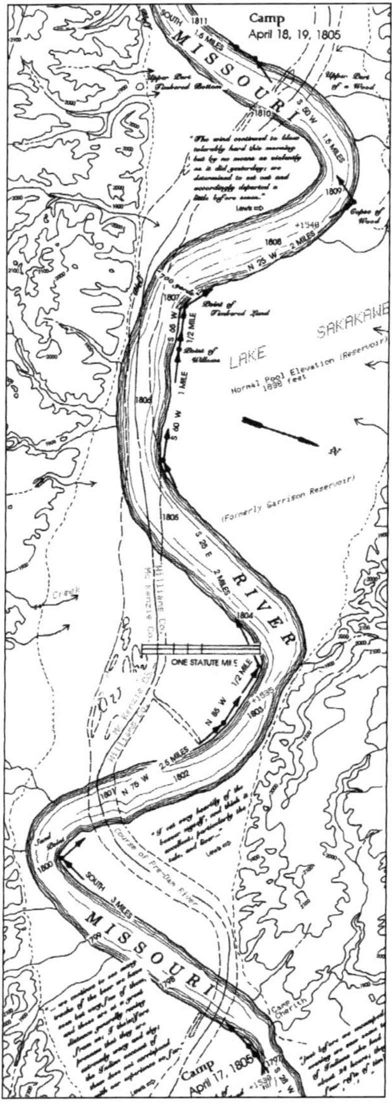

Portion of the route map, above, drawn by William Clark, shows the part of the river traveled between April 16 and 21, 1805. The area inside the faint box corresponds to the cartographic reconstruction at left and the Course and Distance information shown on page 228.

Mapmaking

WILLIAM CLARK WAS THE MAPMAKER. When the expedition left St. Louis in 1804, he took copies of the best maps available. Clark had a large comprehensive map, drafted by Nicholas King in 1803, that had a longitude and latitude grid accurately showing the course of the lower Missouri River as well as the Pacific Coast. Lewis & Clark were expected to fill in the blank area in the middle of the map. Clark also carried copies of maps made by Spanish and French explorers that showed parts of the upper Missouri River region to the Rocky Mountains.

President Jefferson had told Captain Lewis he wanted him to accurately record bearings and courses as the Corps of Discovery traveled west to the Pacific Ocean. But frontier surveying was nowhere near as accurate as ordinary surveying. Rather than a series of closed loop traverses, Clark would have to make do with a single open-ended traverse several thousand miles long.

Ordinary surveying methods, using a transit and chain to create several hundred accurate closed traverses, would be impossible to use on the trip, so shortcuts were developed. Since most of the journey would be on water, Clark tried using a "log line" to measure distances. A log line (a piece of rope of a known length tied to a piece of wood) was used to measure distance and speed of the river. Unfortunately, it did not work well and errors of 25-40% were common. A sighting compass replaced the transit, but errors due to local magnetic anomalies and magnetic declination were common. In the end, Clark resorted to dead reckoning for much of the journey.

Lewis and Clark also used an octant and sextant to try to determine latitude and, with the aid of a chronometer (an accurate timepiece), longitude. Their chronometer stopped several times, and poor weather often made it difficult to make the necessary sightings on stars. Virtually none of those readings were accurate enough to be of any use.

Clark made many map sketches as they traveled across the continent. Those charts laid out the course of the Missouri River and showed many details of the land along the route. Unfortunately, Clark's original maps between St. Louis and Fort Mandan have been lost. After the expedition was completed, Clark allowed Prince Maximilian, a German anthropologist, to copy some maps he had made of the lower Missouri River. Those maps, used during Maximilian's trip up the Missouri in 1833, include 17 sheets (numbered 13 through 29) illustrating the river from Omaha to the Mandan villages in North Dakota. In July 1805, President Jefferson wrote that he had received "29

(on the Lard side) Course Distance &c for
bluff) April 17th 1805.

S. 70. W. 3 Miles to a willow p...
on Stard side –
S. 75. W. ½ m. to a point on St. side op...
N. 75 W. 3 Miles to a wood in a bend to...
N. 50 W. 3½ Miles to a point of woodland on...
S. 65. W. ¾ of a Mile to a point of woodland S.S. op...
to a bluff on Lard side...
above which a creek falls in...
Lard. about 10 yards wide
N. 80 W. 3¼ to a willow point on Lard side
S. 85. W. 3¾ m. Lard point of Woodland
opposite to a bluff on Std. side
passing a creek on Star. at 2 m
W. – – 1 M. along the Lard. point of Woodland
a high bluff on Stard. through
on which a small creek discharges
S. 40. W. 1 along the same point of Woodland Lard.
S. 30. W. ¼ mile along the Lard point to a willow point
S. 14. W. 4 Miles to the upper point of the high
timber on Stard side. —
S. 28. W. 2 ml. to a point on Lard. where
we encamped for the evening

26 Miles.

Part of a page from Clark's daily journal showing his Courses & Distances for April 17, 1805, on the Missouri River just west of the present-day Lewis and Clark State Park in North Dakota. While Clark believed they covered 26 miles that day, they actually traveled only 13 miles. This area is now flooded by Lake Sakakawea, behind Garrison Dam, just west of where Fort Mandan was located.

... coming to life ...

Plamondon's maps make the Expedition journals come to life in a way previously impossible. Remarkably, nobody had ever used Clark's field notes to create a set of maps. Plamondon's third volume charts the route along the Columbia River from Pasco to the Pacific Ocean and back to St. Louis. Gary Moulton, editor of the University of Nebraska edition of the Lewis and Clark journals, also compiled a large volume reproducing all the known maps Clark created during the journey. Those maps, which are often hard to decipher in the original, come to life when viewed in conjunction with the trail maps drawn by Martin Plamondon.

half sheets" from Lewis and Clark at Fort Mandan showing the course of the river to that point, so it is evident the 12 missing maps existed at one time.

In any case, during the winter months of 1805 while at Fort Mandan, Clark created a single map that incorporated everything he knew or believed to be true about the land between the Mississippi River and the Pacific Ocean. His map was based on maps made by other explorers, information supplied by various Indians and fur trappers, and information Clark recorded on their journey up the Missouri in 1804. That map was aboard the keelboat when it returned to St. Louis in 1805. The original "Fort Mandan" map has been lost, but two of the four copies made by Nicholas King in 1805 still exist. While the information obtained from the Indians on the 1805 map was speculative, it proved to be remarkably accurate once the journey was over and the final maps drawn.

The following winter, at Fort Clatsop, Clark consolidated his field notes covering their journey west from Fort Mandan. He made a series of small maps that were used to create a large detailed map after the journey was over. He may have added information to the 1803 "Map of the West" that King had drafted for Clark's use.

Clark kept detailed field notes in his journal showing courses and distances traveled each day. Clark assumed cartographers would use his painstakingly recorded traverse to create accurate maps after the journey was completed. But for almost 200 years, those field notes were ignored. Fortunately, Martin Plamondon II, a resident from Vancouver, Washington, changed all that with his Lewis and Clark Trail Maps.

Martin Plamondon II, a descendent of Southwest Washington pioneer Simon Plamondon, worked for 30 years to create a three-volume set of more than 500 maps covering the entire 7,400 mile route Lewis and Clark took. Sadly, on May 26, 2004, just before his third and final volume was published by Washington State University, Plamondon died. His health had been declining for years and for a while he had been afraid he might not complete his project.

His *Lewis and Clark Trail Maps* are cartographic reconstructions that cover every step of the journey, comparing the rivers as they flowed 200 years ago to their present-day courses. Surprisingly, the contrast is often impressive. Locations of the campsites along with the present day river channels and features, with towns, roads, bridges, dams, etc., added, help modern day explorers retrace the route. Relevant quotations from the expedition journals were added to each map to help the reader understand events the Corps of Discovery experienced.

Thomas Jefferson (1743-1826), by Charles Willson Peale

… Jefferson believed …

Without the vision and curiosity of the third President, Thomas Jefferson, Lewis, Clark and the Expedition would not exist. Jefferson had been interested in the lands west of the Appalachians and Mississippi since the 1780s, having spent time in Europe as U.S. Ambassador to France. Many historians think Jefferson was profoundly influenced by Captain James Cook's "A Voyage to the Pacific Ocean," published in London in 1784.

EPISODE 33

Politics and Destiny

Many CRR readers are frustrated with today's political gridlock and the "do-nothing" Congress in Washington D.C. It seems like it has been impossible to get politicians to work together for America's future over the last couple of decades. So it was illuminating to me as I read the history books to realize modern America's impression of our early Presidents and Congressional leaders might best be described as looking through rose colored glasses! Our "heroes," like George Washington, John Adams, Thomas Jefferson, Alexander Hamilton, James Madison, etc., weren't always viewed as favorably as they are today.

America's first two political parties were beginning to take shape by the 1800 Presidential election. America's second President, John Adams, was a Federalist who narrowly defeated Thomas Jefferson (the Democratic-Republican candidate) in the 1796 election — resulting in Jefferson being Adams's vice president. Prior to 1804, the Presidential candidate who received the second-most Electoral College votes became vice president.

For the 1800 election, Jefferson and Aaron Burr each received 73 electoral votes, so the House of Representatives had to decide which man would become President. After 35 ballots, the vote was still tied. Finally, Alexander Hamilton, America's first Secretary of the Treasury and a well respected Federalist party leader (who hated Aaron Burr more than he despised Thomas Jefferson), convinced a few Federalists to switch their vote, and Jefferson became President and Burr became vice president. If Hamilton hadn't done that, it is quite possible Aaron Burr would have been President, and Jefferson's dream of expanding the United States might never have come to be. For that reason, we should probably consider Alexander Hamilton to be just as important as Thomas Jefferson in the Corps of Discovery.

Like Father, Like Son

Burr was furious at what Hamilton had done, and in 1804, while still vice president, Burr shot and killed Hamilton in a duel! Surprisingly, Burr was not charged for the illegal duel, but he was charged with treason in 1807. Interestingly, Hamilton's 19-year-old son had been killed in the same manner in 1801.

The bitter 1800 election campaign had been characterized by personal attacks and slander. Federalists were convinced the Democrat-Republicans would destroy the country; even George Washington had nothing good to say about the Democrat-Republicans. Much of what has gone on in our recent elections appears tame compared to the dirty dealings of 200 years ago.

A Stretch of the Imagination

In the late 1700s most of the people of the newly-formed United States lived within 50 miles of the Atlantic Ocean. Their idea of the wild west, the frontier, was the relatively unimposing Appalachian Mountains, and the boundary of their imaginations the Mississippi River. Few instances in history offer such proof of the power of curiosity and scientific study as the self-education of Thomas Jefferson and the empowering of his fertile mind by his own readings and musings. For 20 years he pondered the reports of traders, explorers, governments and diplomats. Yet the stretch of the imagination was primarily his, and it stretched the boundaries of our frontiers, and our country, immeasurably.

Jefferson Memorial, Washington, D.C.

A hidden agenda?

As I read the dozens of books I bought during the Bicentennial of the Corps of Discovery's epic journey, I was fascinated to learn more about how Thomas Jefferson was able to fulfill his vision of expanding the United States. The 1803 Louisiana Purchase actually occurred a year after Jefferson created the Corps of Discovery. I always assumed Jefferson and Congress were extraordinary visionaries to be willing to explore the western lands and expand the country just 25 years after the Declaration of Independence was signed. But after reading countless books, I now realize it was a miracle any of this happened.

Surrounded by bitter political dissension in 1801, Jefferson needed a private secretary he could trust. He remembered Meriwether Lewis who had grown up a few miles from the Jefferson estate at Monticello. But most people found it hard to know what Jefferson saw in the young man known to be moody, serious and awkward. Letters Lewis wrote show that, despite a good education, his grammar was dubious and it was evident he was never going to be a good speller (his journals prove that!). None of these deficiencies bothered Jefferson; he saw in Lewis a man capable of carrying out some very special duties.

Jefferson had not reached the point of publicly admitting his plans in 1801, but he had been dreaming for 20 years of exploring the vast lands west of the Mississippi River. Jefferson, who never traveled more than 50 miles from his Monticello estate (except for five years in Paris as Minister to France), wanted to take the fur trade from the British, and expand America all the way to the Pacific Ocean.

Jefferson had been trying to get support from the government to explore the western part of North America since at least 1780, but his position as Secretary of State was not enough to win Congressional or party support. At age 18, Lewis had begged Jefferson to let him join a proposed 1792 expedition to explore the uncharted west; that scheme, like several before, was abandoned due to lack of governmental interest.

However, when Jefferson became President, he had the power to send out the explorers if he could get Congress to appropriate some money. He knew Congress wouldn't willingly fund such an expedition, so he had to keep the true intent secret. Jefferson immediately wrote to Lewis and offered him the job as his secretary. The letter was written so it was plain enough to Lewis what Jefferson really wanted, but nobody else would understand. Lewis immediately accepted, and the rest is history. Four years later, Captain Lewis would fulfill Jefferson's dream, and forever lock in America's claim to the land west of the Mississippi River.

BIOGRAPHICAL SKETCHES

MICHAEL O. PERRY

Mike Perry wears the title of amateur historian proudly. He is intensely curious about the natural world, and worked as an environmental technician for the Weyerhaeuser Company. A lifelong explorer, observer and collector, he has compiled extensive coin and stamp collections, and maintains a personal library of more than 1,300 historical picture postcards portraying the Lower Columbia region. Mike has served as president of the Cowlitz County Historical Society Board of Directors and volunteered at an outdoor school on the Cispus River in Washington's Cascade Mountains. A native of Longview, Washington, he lives with his wife, Marilyn Perry, in Kelso,Washington. This is his first book.

DEBBY NEELY

A student and teacher of the printmaking arts, Debby Neely remains particularly smitten by the woodcut. "I sign my name with the red chops. The top chop is my name in Chinese. The bottom chop says I draw birds and animals." This is her second collaboration with Columbia River Reader Press.

HAL CALBOM

A journalist, educator, and filmmaker, Hal Calbom writes and photographs the monthly "People+Place" feature for Columbia River Reader. He is author of "Resourceful: Leadership and Communication in a Relationship Age," and winner of five Emmy Awards for film production.

SUSAN PERRY PIPER

Since 2004, Susan Piper has edited and published Columbia River Reader, a monthly literary and lifestyle publication, personally shaping the design, editorial and advertising content of more than 180 issues. She co-founded Columbia River Reader Press in 2018.

COLUMBIA RIVER READER PRESS

CRR Press is a subsidiary of Columbia River Reader, LLC. www.crreader.com/CRRPress.

Paintings

"Lewis and Clark,"1804 © by L. Edward Fisher
and commissioned by the Missouri Bankers Association.
Hanging at the James C. Kirkpatrick State Information Center, Jefferson City, Missouri

"York,"
"Lewis and Clark Meeting Indians at Ross' Hole"
"Lewis and Clark Reach the Shoshone Camp Led by Sacajawea"
by Charles M. Russell, C.M. *Russell Museum, Great Falls, Montana*

"Bird's Eye View of A Mandan Village," by George Catlin
Smithsonian American Art Museum, Washington, D.C.

"The Interior of a Mandan Hut," by Karl Bodmer
Gilcrease Museum, Tulsa, Oklahoma

"The Salt Makers," by John F. Claymer
Clymer Museum of Art, Ellensburg, Washington

Portraits of
Meriwether Lewis,
William Clark, and Thomas Jefferson
by Charles Willson Peale
Independence National Historical Park Collection, Philadelphia, Pennsylvania

Portrait of Nicholas Biddle by William Inman
Atwater Kent Museum, Philadelphia, Pennsylvania

A NOTE ABOUT TYPE

Dispatches from the Discovery Trail is set in Goudy Old Style, designed by Frederic W. Goudy in Birmingham, England, in the 1750s; and Century Gothic, based on Monotype 20th Century, which was drawn by Sol Hess between 1936 and 1947. The publisher first encountered and developed an affinity for these particular type families in 1996 under the tutelage of Leslie Waygren, the revered "Font Maven" at University of Oregon's Electronic Publishing Program.

ACKNOWLEDGMENTS

With gratitude to our father, the late George O. Perry, for instilling in us the love of books, an appreciation for local history, the enjoyment of our majestic Pacific Northwest, and awe at the wonders of the world.

~ *Michael O. Perry and Susan Perry Piper*

Woodcuts by Debby Neely:

"Whispering" (cover)
"Heron" (frontispiece)
"Great Horned Owl" (The Vision)
"Otter" (The River)
"Raven II with Moon" (The Divide)
"Sturgeon" (The Sea)
"Redwing" (The Return)
"North Fork Chinook" (The Legacy)
"Snipe" (end cut)
"Meadowlark" (back cover)

IMAGES

CRRPress has followed the Fair Use Doctrine, and Wikimedia Commons {{PD-Art}} license protocols for images which are in the Public Domain due to their age. Current locations of the original paintings are listed on the facing page. Other images: Harper's Ferry National Historical Park and Lewis & Clark National Historical Park, National Parks Service and Bureau of Land Management, U.S. Department of the Interior; U.S. Army Corps. of Engineers; Oregon Historical Society; U.S. Mint and Bureau of Engraving and Printing, Department of the Treasury; U.S. Postal Service.

Reproductions from the authentic journals of Lewis and Clark used with the permission from the American Philosophical Society, and with gratitude to Charles B. Greifenstein.

The author and editors have made every effort to ensure historical accuracy, correctly attribute quotations, and cite provenance and credit for the use of images and illustrations. We apologize for any errors, omissions, or misstatements of facts which are solely our responsibility.

COLUMBIA RIVER READER PRESS

We are celebrators, curators and custodians of the Lower Columbia River region of the Pacific Northwest — its history, culture, and art.

Columbia River Reader Press is a subsidiary of Columbia River Reader, LLC, which produces a literary and lifestyle publication distributed monthly in the Lower Columbia region in Washington and Oregon States. The Reader has steadily expanded its distribution and advertising base, and in 2018 announced expansion plans which included launching Columbia River Reader Press, and initiated a yearly subscription service and online store, the CRR Collector's Club.

CRRPress published *The Tidewater Reach: Field Guide to the Lower Columbia River in Poems and Pictures*, by Robert Michael Pyle and Judy VanderMaten, in early 2020. *Tidewater Reach* is in its second printing and is presented in both a Signature Edition, in color, with artists' autographs; and a black and white, trade paperback edition. Both feature an imaginative integration of verses and images and an extended interview with the author, a beloved Pacific Northwest naturalist and writer.

Dispatches from the Discovery Trail compiles and amplifies a popular series run in the Reader since its inception. *Dispatches* author Michael O. Perry chronicles the Lewis and Clark Expedition from a journalistic, layman's point of view, adding additional illustrations and commentary.

CRRPress also distributes select works which amplify its mission and cater to the interests of its readers. First among these are three books by regional author Rex Ziak, who revolutionized Lewis and Clark scholarship and changed the historical record: *In Full View; Eyewitness to Astoria;* and *Lewis and Clark Down and Up the Columbia River.*

For ordering and subscription information, see the following page or order online at crreader.com/crrpress.

CRRPress books are also available in custom editions suitable for particular audiences. For additional information please contact:

Columbia River Reader Press
1333 14th Avenue, Longview, WA 98632
email: publisher@crreader.com

COLUMBIA RIVER READER PRESS

COLUMBIA RIVER READER COLLECTORS CLUB

DISPATCHES FROM THE DISCOVERY TRAIL
by Michael O. Perry

THE TIDEWATER REACH
by Robert Michael Pyle & Judy VanderMaten

BOOKS BY REX ZIAK

☐ *Columbia River Reader 11-issue subscription starting with next issue. For gift subscriptions, include name, mailing address; gift announcement card will be sent.*
___@ $55 = __________

☐ *Dispatches from the Discovery Trail (Color and B/W) Boxed Signature Edition* ___ @ $50 = __________

☐ *Dispatches from the Discovery Trail (B/W) Trade Paperback* ___ @ $25 = __________

☐ *The Tidewater Reach (Color and B/W) Boxed Signature Edition* ___ @ $50 = __________

☐ *The Tidewater Reach (B/W) Trade Paperback* ___ @ $25 = __________

☐ *In Full View* ___ @ $30 = __________

☐ *Eyewitness to Astoria* ___ @ $22 = __________

☐ *Lewis and Clark Down and Up the Columbia River* ___ @ $19 = __________

Sub-Total __________

Washington residents add sales tax 8.1%__________

Book Orders: Add Shipping & Handling $ 3.90

TOTAL __________

Please enclose check payable to CRR Press; to pay via credit card, please call 360-749-1021 or visit www.crreader.com/crrpress.

CRR Press
1333 14th Ave.
Longview, WA 98632

Name __________________________

Street __________________________

City/State/Zip __________________________

email __________________________

Phone __________________________

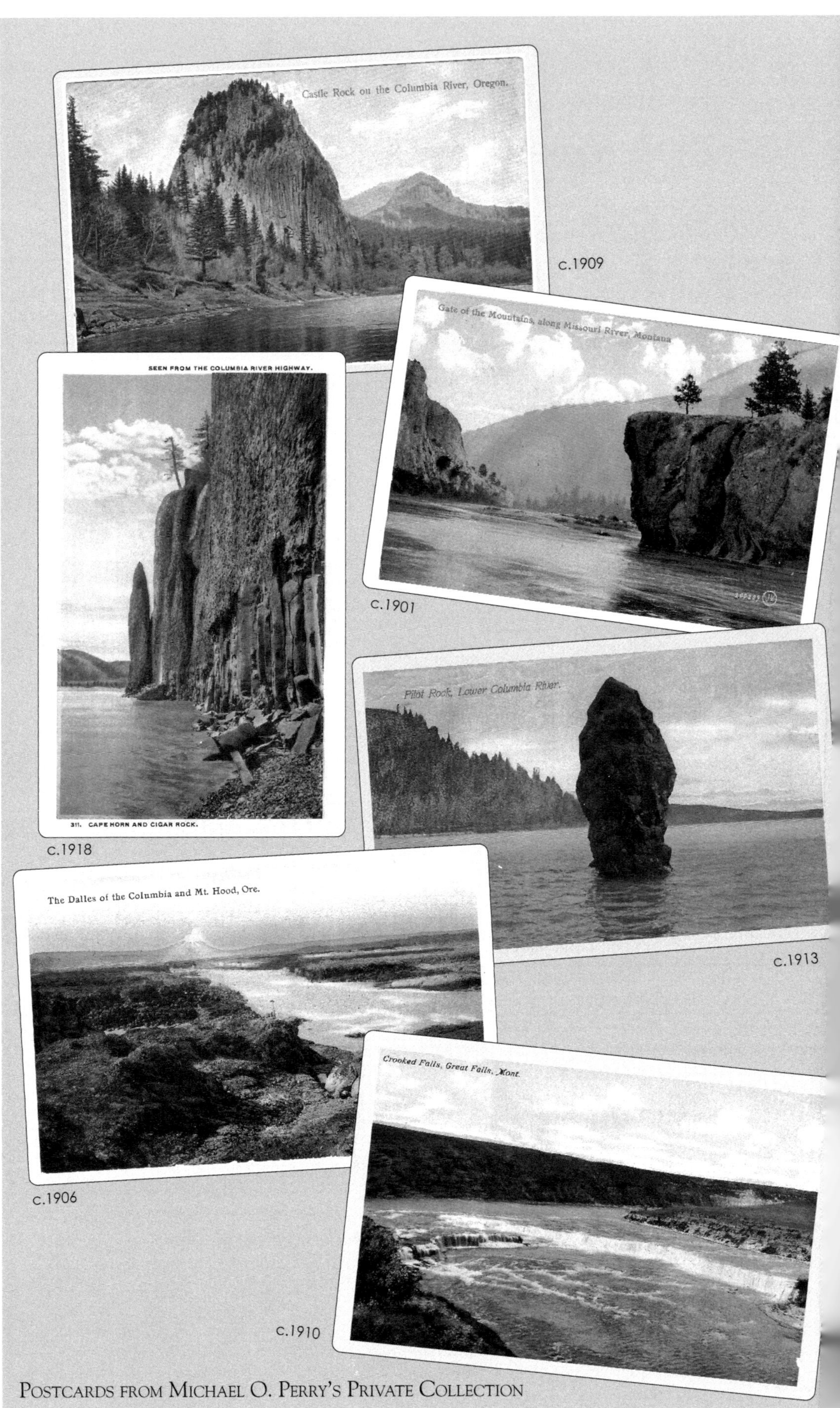

Castle Rock on the Columbia River, Oregon.
c.1909
Gate of the Mountains, along Missouri River, Montana
c.1901
SEEN FROM THE COLUMBIA RIVER HIGHWAY.
311. CAPE HORN AND CIGAR ROCK.
c.1918
Pilot Rock, Lower Columbia River.
c.1913
The Dalles of the Columbia and Mt. Hood, Ore.
c.1906
Crooked Falls, Great Falls, Mont.
c.1910

Postcards from Michael O. Perry's Private Collection

A Conversation
with
Michael O. Perry

Hal Calbom

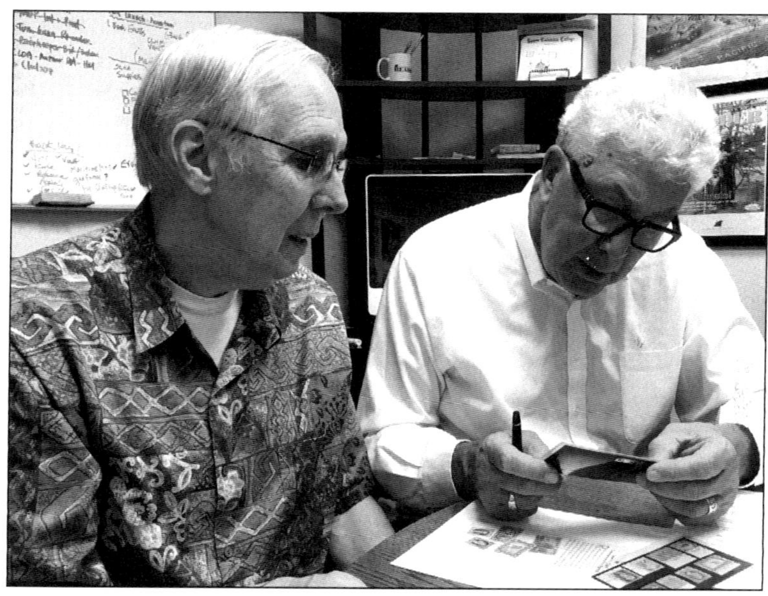

Michael O. Perry and Hal Calbom, Longview, Washington, September 2020

THE LAYMAN'S LEWIS & CLARK: MICHAEL O. PERRY

Michael Perry has two complementary traits. He's curious, with wide interests. And to satisfy that curiosity, he can be thorough. To the point of, dare we say, obsession.

As an environmental technician at Weyerhaeuser Company, he measured air and water quality and filed meticulous monthly reports required by the company and its regulators. As a collector since boyhood, he's amassed albums full of stamps. And as an amateur historian he prizes hundreds of postcards illustrating the early history of the Lower Columbia region.

Some 20 years ago, with retirement looming, Michael Perry got an interesting offer. A colleague had just purchased a local newspaper, the Columbia River Reader, and wanted a series of articles following the upcoming bicentennial of the Lewis and Clark Expedition. Might the curious collector have an interest?

"Dispatch from the Discovery Trail" premiered in Columbia River Reader April 15, 2004, following the Expedition's timeline for 33 months and documenting its commemoration. Two re-printings later, it remains the most popular series ever run by the Reader, which both delights and amazes its author.

MP: I didn't really know where it was going when I started. I was just hoping I could keep up with it.

HC: One piece a month? How long?

MP: One piece a month, six or seven hundred words, more or less tracking their progress for the whole expedition, over two and a half years, stage by stage. So, I went out and bought the Moulton edition of the Lewis and Clark Journals, and it scared the daylights out of me! I mean it's about a foot and a half long set of books, and you start reading that and you realize these haven't been edited for the casual reader. Any reader, for that matter.

HC: Aren't there interpretive books, too?

MP: Oh yes, dozens of them. But they're all over the place. And as regional author Rex Ziak found out — a guy that really influenced this project, and all the expedition scholarship, really — some of them are just flat wrong. It's just a lot of material, a ton of material, and it's based largely on these very raw journal entries.

HC: Did you use some of the other journals, besides Lewis's and Clark's?

MP: Yes, and in some ways the journals of the corpsmen were more interesting — they didn't have the burden of naming and classifying everything, following Jefferson's really precise instructions.

HC: But the journals remain your primary sources?

MP: Yes, but with exceptions. They're literally hard to read, and they've been mis-read and misinterpreted. But I also wanted to find things people today might be interested in. I said, 'What can I pull out of here that is different? That might have happened this month two hundred years ago?'

HC: Give me an example.

MP: Well, there's all this time, a lot of time, when not much is going on but hard, hard work. Just trying to get up the Missouri River is agony. But guys are also sneaking off to get whiskey, and they'd be punished with actual beatings, 50 lashes sometimes, which appalled the Indians, by the way. So I picked up on those types of things that interested me, not a scholar, just someone who might see this all from a different view. Things that hadn't been given a lot of attention perhaps.

HC: So you were looking for the significance of things, not just the events? The stories, maybe?

MP: Yes, I think that's a fair statement. In this case, we need to remember this was a military expedition under military rules, and people were subjected to some pretty tough discipline and punishment. Probably why they all survived.

Back in 2003 and 2004 the country went to great lengths to commemorate Lewis and Clark. But like the Expedition itself, the Bicentennial spawned mixed results and messages. The Corps of Discovery has always confounded an overarching narrative. Mike Perry's division into 33 installments is as useful a way as any to piece together a story that remains fundamentally episodic, a series of dramatic moments strung together with sweat and perseverance but lacking a central story line. Many of its landmarks are lost to the contemporary viewer or traveler, and inevitably modern "commemorations" devolved into local or regional events highlighting various dramatic links in the huge, and unwieldy, narrative chain. Those looking for a sense of the whole — intention, meaning, significance — are frustrated from its very inception.

MP: I think we always tend to think that everything that was discovered was discovered by an American. Down deep we knew the Spanish had been here forever, and the Russians. Look at all the Russian settlements in Alaska and California, and the French and the English presence.

HC: Were you actively trying to correct the historical record?

MP: Not at all. This information was all there already, I simply shined a light on it. And I have the luxury of not being a professional historian. I find things I'm curious about, interested in, and hopefully the readers share that curiosity. So we find out the Alexander Mackenzie had made the trip across the continent in the 1790s, 1793 or whenever, and didn't even bother writing about it for eight years. And finally Jefferson reads it for the first time in 1802, I believe it was. And he's been wanting to do this for fifteen years, even when he was a relative nobody. And that plants the seed for the expedition.

HC: You start the series with a couple of pretty bold statements, that Jefferson basically deceived congress in planning and funding the trip?

MP: Jefferson kept trying to stir up interest for the project, and finally when he became president he wrote a letter to Lewis, a cryptic letter, telling him that we're going to do this and you're the man, but we can't tell anybody because this was against the law.

HC: How so?

MP: We're invading a foreign territory, owned — he thought at the time — by Spain. But in the meantime — and of course everything takes months or more likely years to be communicated — Spain has ceded it back to France. And there's no way Jefferson wants Napoleon owning that huge piece of North America, so when he finds this out he sends representatives to France with authorization to try to buy New Orleans and as much of the Mississippi Valley as they can get.

HC: And France is in a spending mood?

MP: One of those miracles of history. Napoleon needs money to fight continental wars, and sells all of Louisiana for $15 million, about $0.03 an acre. So the ground shifts, literally, and all of a sudden Lewis and his party become trade representatives and surveyors rather than foreign invaders. Jefferson still equips them with French and Spanish passports, too, just in case.

HC:: And lest we forget "Louisiana" was considerably bigger than the state that bears its name today.

MP: From the Mississippi to the Rockies, and from the Mexican to the Canadian borders. But Jefferson continued to have ambitions beyond that. That's where he came up with another convenient fiction, that the purpose of the Expedition was to find the water route from Atlantic to Pacific.

HC:: The fabled Northwest Passage.

MP: Yes, but — spoiler alert — trappers and traders and the Indians themselves had known for years there was no contiguous route from east to west, and by the time Lewis and Clark had wintered at Ft. Mandan, and talked to all these people, they knew it, too.

HC: But didn't the Purchase make it easier to justify the expedition?

MP: It did, with limits drawn around it. The purchase made it easier for Jefferson to get the money from Congress, because trade came to the fore. He wanted to go out and establish relations with the Indians and let them know that we're the new owner of the land, and to quit trading with the British and the French, because our people are coming out. Our businesspeople will come out and set up the trading posts. But still, the Congress's instructions said you can only go as far as the drainage of the Missouri. Going to the ocean was not something they contemplated or authorized.

Three years after their homecoming, William Clark learned that his partner Lewis had been shot dead, most likely by his own hand, in a forlorn Tennessee lodging house called Grinder's Stand. Clark would come to mourn more than his 35-year-old former co-captain. He had waited three years for Lewis to pen the grand tale of their exploits, and entrusted him with all his own journals and maps — three years for the grand summing up, the immortalizing, clarifying conclusion. Instead, to his chagrin (and we assume that of Thomas Jefferson as well), Lewis had written not a single word. There would be no definitive history, at least in the first person. In the subsequent years the professors, publicists and pundits have all had their cracks at it, but in truth they, and we, still rely on those obscure primary sources — the patchwork of scrawled observations in the journals. It's a history that remains uniquely open-ended and still evolving. It sprawls over three years and four thousand miles, and two centuries. It remains, literally, an open book.

MP: It was good discipline to have to write 1,000 words a month, and write them for the lay reader. I could look for things that you might not read in the history books — footnotes, asides, items of interest to someone just giving it a glance. Something I might get out of my car and investigate myself.

HC: How about your personal takeaways? What did you feel like you learned or stuck with you after all this reading and viewing and work?

MP: The toughness of these very ordinary men. They went the whole route, loyal to the end, never complaining. And this was dangerous, backbreaking, scary stuff. Down there at the mouth of the Columbia dodging six foot diameter logs, marooned between a rock cliff and the tides and storms pelting you. And starving in the mountains. It's real hardship. And yet, when they got back, they simply went back to their ordinary lives.

HC: No grand parades?

MP: No, the outcomes of the Expedition, I think, are somewhat disappointing. Besides Lewis's failing to write it all up, nobody published Clark's maps. The natural history studies, drawings and descriptions and discoveries, got filed away in some obscure place. And, of course the politics and diplomacy just went on and on, pretty oblivious. So, really the most important thing they accomplished was reinforcing our claim to the land, which wouldn't get settled with Great Britain until years later, anyway.

HC: How about your personal journey, what stays with you?

MP: The closest I got to walking in their tracks was the portages around Great Falls. And I literally got down in those ravines, with that prickly pear cactus everywhere, and walked it all. The ground is so hard, and the buffalo had made hoof prints which had hardened into sharp edges, and these guys trudged across in their moccasins, falling asleep where they stood, as I mentioned in the narrative. That was a powerful moment for me.

HC: Thoughts for your readers, takeaways for them, perhaps?

MP: We just need to slow down and smell the roses in life. That's history. I remember I got a note from a lady who said, after reading one of my "Postmarks along the Trail" — a series I wrote after Dispatches — she loaded her teddy bear in the car with a copy of the Reader and took all the back roads to Vancouver. She said thank you so much, it was the most enjoyable thing. History is that way. There is more out there than we can possibly learn. These little towns around here that we all hear the names but don't know anything of. Why were they there, and what went on? If I can share those things that's the most rewarding.

HC: Take more of the "blue highways," as they're often called?

MP: You remember Charles Kuralt? He did a piece when they finished our interstate highway system. And finished up on camera and said something like, "Well, the news is today the interstate highway system is complete. It's now possible to drive coast to coast and not see a thing."

Portions of this interview originated in Columbia River Reader, Oct. and Nov./Dec. issues 2020.
Interviews are edited for length and condensed for clarity, Copyright MMXX • Columbia River Reader

LIBERTY
IN GOD WE TRUST
2000
UNITED STATES OF AMERICA
E PLURIBUS UNUM
ONE DOLLAR
1804
UNITED STATES POSTAGE
2004
LEWIS & CLARK BICENTENNIAL
37
CENTS
CLARK
LEWIS
UNITED STATES OF AMERICA
POSTAGE
TEN CENTS
10
THE UNITED STATES OF AMERICA
TEN DOLLARS
TEN
UNITED STATES NOTE
IN GOD WE TRUST
Liberty
2005
FIVE CENTS
PEACE
AND
FRIENDSHIP
UNITED
OF AMERICA
FIVE
SILVER CERTIFICATE
5
ONE DOLLAR
LEWIS & CLARK
LEWIS AND CLARK EXPEDITION
1804
1954
UNITED STATES POSTAGE 3¢
1935
FIVE CENTS

Columbia River Reader Press